Cambridge Elements

Elements in Current Archaeological Tools and Techniques
edited by
Hans Barnard
Cotsen Institute of Archaeology
Willeke Wendrich
Polytechnic University of Turin

CERAMIC ANALYSIS

Laboratory Methods

Irmgard Hein
University of Vienna

Mustafa Kibaroğlu
University of Tübingen

Michaela Schauer
University of Vienna

Anno Hein
Institute of Nanoscience and Nanotechnology, NCSR "Demokritos"

Georgios S. Polymeris
Institute of Nanoscience and Nanotechnology, NCSR "Demokritos"

Judit Molera
University of Vic – Central University of Catalonia

Trinitat Pradell
Polytechnic University of Catalonia

Shaftesbury Road, Cambridge CB2 8EA, United Kingdom

One Liberty Plaza, 20th Floor, New York, NY 10006, USA

477 Williamstown Road, Port Melbourne, VIC 3207, Australia

314–321, 3rd Floor, Plot 3, Splendor Forum, Jasola District Centre, New Delhi – 110025, India

103 Penang Road, #05–06/07, Visioncrest Commercial, Singapore 238467

Cambridge University Press is part of Cambridge University Press & Assessment, a department of the University of Cambridge.

We share the University's mission to contribute to society through the pursuit of education, learning and research at the highest international levels of excellence.

www.cambridge.org
Information on this title: www.cambridge.org/9781009530750

DOI: 10.1017/9781009530774

© Irmgard Hein, Mustafa Kibaroğlu, Michaela Schauer, Anno Hein, Georgios S. Polymeris, Judit Molera and Trinitat Pradell 2025

This publication is in copyright. Subject to statutory exception and to the provisions of relevant collective licensing agreements, no reproduction of any part may take place without the written permission of Cambridge University Press & Assessment.

When citing this work, please include a reference to the DOI 10.1017/9781009530774

First published 2025

A catalogue record for this publication is available from the British Library

ISBN 978-1-009-53075-0 Hardback
ISBN 978-1-009-53078-1 Paperback
ISSN 2632-7031 (online)
ISSN 2632-7023 (print)

Cambridge University Press & Assessment has no responsibility for the persistence or accuracy of URLs for external or third-party internet websites referred to in this publication and does not guarantee that any content on such websites is, or will remain, accurate or appropriate.

For EU product safety concerns, contact us at Calle de José Abascal, 56, 1°, 28003 Madrid, Spain, or email eugpsr@cambridge.org

Ceramic Analysis

Laboratory Methods

Elements in Current Archaeological Tools and Techniques

DOI: 10.1017/9781009530774
First published online: August 2025

Irmgard Hein
University of Vienna

Mustafa Kibaroğlu
University of Tübingen

Michaela Schauer
University of Vienna

Anno Hein
Institute of Nanoscience and Nanotechnology, NCSR "Demokritos"

Georgios S. Polymeris
Institute of Nanoscience and Nanotechnology, NCSR "Demokritos"

Judit Molera
University of Vic – Central University of Catalonia

Trinitat Pradell
Polytechnic University of Catalonia

Author for correspondence: Irmgard Hein, irmgard.hein@univie.ac.at

Abstract: This Element, authored by a team of specialist researchers, provides an overview of the various analytical techniques employed in the laboratory for the examination of archaeological ceramic materials. Pottery represents one of the earliest technical materials used by humans and is arguably the most frequently encountered object in archaeological sites. The original plastic raw material, which is solidified by firing, exhibits a wide range of variations in terms of production methods, material, form, decoration, and function. This frequently presents significant challenges for archaeologists. In modern laboratories, a variety of archaeometric measurement methods are available for addressing a wide range of archaeological questions. Examples of these include determining the composition of archaeological materials, elucidating the processes involved in manufacturing and decoration, estimating the age of archaeological material, and much more. The six sections present available methods for analysing pottery, along with an exploration of their potential application.

Keywords: age assessment, ceramic analysis, archaeometrical methods, ceramic technology, ceramic properties

© Irmgard Hein, Mustafa Kibaroğlu, Michaela Schauer, Anno Hein, Georgios S. Polymeris, Judit Molera and Trinitat Pradell 2025

ISBNs: 9781009530750 (HB), 9781009530781 (PB), 9781009530774 (OC)
ISSNs: 2632-7031 (online), 2632-7023 (print)

Contents

1 Introduction 1
  Irmgard Hein & Michaela Schauer

2 Visualization Methods, Microstructural, Mineralogical, and Chemical Analysis 3
  Mustafa Kibaroğlu & Michaela Schauer

3 Material Testing of Pottery 21
  Anno Hein

4 The Firing 26
  Anno Hein

5 Thermoluminescence as a Tool for Age Assessment and Palaeothermometry Studies of Baked Clayey Artefacts 32
  Georgios S. Polymeris

6 Specific Types of Ceramics: Analysis of Glazed Surfaces 48
  Judit Molera & Trinitat Pradell

7 Further Surface Treatments 61
  Anno Hein

8 Statistical Approaches to the Evaluation of Analytical Data in Ceramic Studies 64
  Anno Hein

References 67

1 Introduction

Irmgard Hein & Michaela Schauer

Fired clay materials (ceramics) are one of the first engineering materials processed by humans. Due to its broad range of use, which encompasses building materials, containers for storage, transport, food preparation, and feasting, as well as luxury items and rituals, ceramic represents one of the most significant artefact categories within the material remains of past societies. Those objects provide insights into the economic organization, trade, cultural interactions, and ritual practices, as well as being crucial for dating cultural layers. This Element focuses on the analysis of the material properties of ceramics, how to define them with laboratory methods, and how to draw archaeological relevant conclusions from the results. The production process and the possibilities of analysis of pottery in the field will be the subject of a subsequent publication in this series.

As perhaps the most plastic of all known media of material culture in prehistory and antiquity, ceramics exhibit enormous variation in terms of production methods, fabric, shape, decoration, and function, offering both tremendous advantages and challenges for the archaeologist. Properties of plastic clay paste were already explored from shaping figurines and solidifying them by placing them in or close to an open fire in central Europe in the Gravettien (ca. 30.700 BC; Soffer et al. 2000). The earliest finds of ceramic vessels are so far from hunter-gatherer contexts in the Paleolithic of southern China (ca. 17.000 BC, Budja 2011) and in Japan (c. 13.000 BC, Kuzmin 2015). Pottery vessel manufacture is then observed with the Meso- and Neolithic in a variety of regions, often in a context of transition from hunter-gatherers to agricultural societies, living in settlements, practicing plant cultivation and livestock farming (Pampuch 2014). The changing human lifestyle through the development of new diets and/or sedentism probably facilitated the invention and spread of pottery technology.

In addition to the production of vessels and tools, ceramic technology also had an impact on the production of durable building materials for the construction of dwellings (mud bricks or adobes, which were simply dried in the sun), starting from c. 7500 BC in the Zagros region (Schmandt-Besserat 1977). The widespread use of fired bricks is documented only much later in the ancient Near East, at approximately 1500 BC. As a consequence of the firing process, the bricks display greater toughness and durability (Pampuch 2014).

Ceramics as a subject of investigation in archaeometry serves to discuss various archaeological questions that vary depending on the archaeological context (Rice 1987; Quinn 2022). As a prerequisite for creating a systematic record of the wide range of artefacts, archaeologists must classify ceramics into groups of similar objects, according to material properties and typology. The literature on archaeological classification of ceramics is vast, but useful overviews may be found in Rice (1987) and Sinopoli (1991), and will be discussed in the upcoming Element 'Ceramic Analysis: Field Methods' in more detail. With the rise of absolute dating methods in the second half of the 20th century, archaeological studies of ceramics have shifted somewhat, with less emphasis on classification, seriation, and chronology construction, in favour of new approaches. This includes detailed physical and chemical analyses of the material composition and manufacturing techniques. Obtaining information in this way also provides insights into the origin, function, distribution, and life span.

In regard to material studies and properties, archaeological ceramics are broadly defined as fired clay and can be viewed as an artificial, intentionally fired, fine-grained sedimentary rock. Its primary constituent, clay, is derived from the weathering of various rock types, more precisely from the alteration of rock-forming minerals such as feldspars, mica, and mafic minerals. They are predominantly transported by fluvial systems and deposited in diverse sedimentary environments. These clay deposits comprise complex constituents, mainly composed of formed clay minerals (due to weathering), clay-sized particles (<0.002 mm), and coarser grains (typically sand-sized: 0.0625–2 mm) of minerals such as quartz, feldspar, or pyroxene, and rock fragments. Consequently, the material properties and composition of ceramics are affected by a spectrum of factors, from the parent rocks through deposition to the human action of production which can also alter the composition by adding temper or changes during the firing process: Through the application of heat the material properties of the clay material is altered completely and irreversibly by transforming the initially plastic clay paste into a solid and primarily brittle ceramic object with basic resistance against mechanical and thermal loads. More on the aspects of production (*chaîne opératoire*) and ways to investigate the material and thermomechanical properties of pottery are given in Sections 3 and 4.

The intricate compositional nature of ceramics is the subject of investigations through an array of analytical techniques, aiding reconstruction of ceramics' history from their material origins and manufacturing processes to their final use. In this endeavour, archaeometry employs a wide range of techniques and methodologies initially developed across various scientific disciplines, especially within physics, chemistry, and geosciences. A selection of analytical methods to gain insight into the composition and therefore production techniques, distribution networks, and origin of archaeological pottery are introduced in Section 2.

Dating of pottery is another very important aspect in the modern analysis of pottery. In many excavations, periodization, namely the indirect dating, is based on the ceramics relative chronology defined by typology. Nevertheless, in many cases the application of a direct dating technique is either required or suggested. Section 5 focuses therefore on the method of thermoluminescence; besides being the most reliable dating technique of fired clay artefacts, it provides useful information regarding the (maximum) firing temperature in the past.

The more elaborate techniques such as polish, slips, clay, or colouring applications or even the sophisticated technique of glazing of ceramics are, on the other hand, specific surface treatments of pottery which are considered in Sections 6 and 7. Studying ancient ceramic glazes helps to understand past technological advances and cultural exchanges. It reveals how people developed technical skills, traded materials, and adopted new trends. By examining ancient glazes, more can be learned about our history and preserve valuable traditions for future generations. Finally, a brief synthesis is given on the statistical methods which are applicable for the interpretation of the analytical results in Section 8.

2 Visualization Methods, Microstructural, Mineralogical, and Chemical Analysis

Mustafa Kibaroğlu & Michaela Schauer

The selection of analytical methods for ceramic investigation may be guided by various factors, including the research question, material characteristics, sample availability and size, resource constraints (time, funding, personnel), and equipment accessibility. The techniques employed in archaeometric ceramics studies can be broadly clustered into three groups:

(1) visualization methods, (2) mineralogical analysis, and (3) chemical analysis. Next, a brief overview is presented of a selection of commonly employed methods in archaeometric study, categorized by each respective area.

2.1 Methods of Visualization and Microtextural Analysis

2.1.1 Petrographic Analysis

Petrographic analysis, also known as thin-section analysis or optical microscopy, is a conventional, yet powerful, analytical technique extensively employed in the scientific investigation of archaeological ceramics. The analysis is carried out on a thin section, which is examined under a special microscope, the so-called polarized light microscope. A thin section is a thin, flat slice with typically 0.03 mm thick, cut from a ceramic sample and mounted onto a glass slide using a specific epoxy resin. The principles of petrographic analysis are based on the identification of mineral inclusions through their known optical properties. Under the microscope, the so-called rock-forming minerals, which are usually the main components of the inclusions, display specific optical properties such as birefringence, pleochroism, twinning, relief, extinction, and other optical features, each unique to a particular mineral type (Figure 1a-d). These diagnostic features facilitate the precise identification of the individual minerals. Similarly, based on these principles, rock fragments that may be included in ceramics can also be identified.

The analysis involves a qualitative examination of the composition of mineral and rock fragments, as well as the micro-textural features of ceramic fabric. This is a rapid, cost-effective, and widely available method, serving as a valuable tool for the archaeometric investigation of ancient ceramic materials. It is particularly capable of examining a wide range of material properties, especially in coarse-grained ceramics. Although this method can be applied to explore various archaeological questions, a common focus in many studies using petrography is determining the geographic origin of the production place of the vessels. This is the only method that enables the identification of rock inclusions in ceramics. Through this method, it is possible to precisely assign the raw material source used in ceramics to a specific area or geological unit, especially in cases where specific rock types are included in the ceramics (Kibaroğlu & Thumm-Doğrayan 2013).

Another main aspect of petrographic analysis is the reconstruction of production processes. The microscopic observation of microtextural features, such as grain size, quantity, shape, and distribution, along with other features like grain orientation, is important for gaining information about the techniques used in production. This may include the material properties of the clay, the strategy for resource choice, and the specific processing techniques applied to the clay paste, such as tempering or purification of raw clay. Petrographic observations

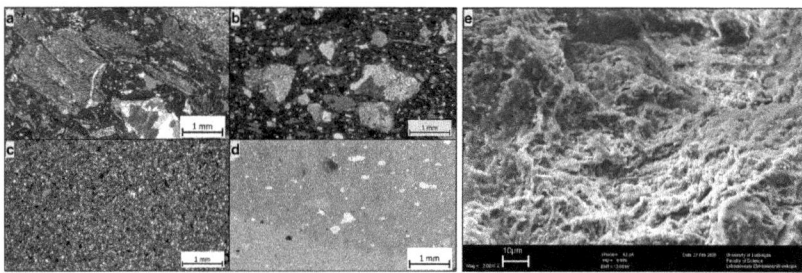

Figure 1 Examples of thin-section photomicrographs of different types of ceramic materials: (a) Late Bronze Age coarse ware from Central Anatolia. (b) Late Chalcolithic coarse ware from Seville, Spain. (c) Early Bronze Age fine ware from Northern Mesopotamia. (d) Early Bronze Age fine ware from Southeastern Anatolia. (e) SEM image of Late Bronze Age ceramic from Plain Cilicia, Southern Anatolia.

can also provide insight into the shaping techniques of vessels (Thér 2016). Furthermore, matrix features such as the optical behaviour of the clay matrix (whether it is optically active or inactive), the degree of vitrification, and the size and morphology of voids are also useful for estimating firing conditions (Braekmans & Degryse 2017). By combining petrographic examinations with other mineralogical techniques like Scanning Electron Microscopy (SEM) or X-ray Diffraction (XRD), more accurate information regarding production technology can be obtained.

The insights gained from such analysis can significantly contribute to our understanding of past societies by providing information on the production places of questioned ceramic groups, manufacturing techniques, technological advancements, trade patterns, cultural interactions, and socioeconomic dynamics. Its cost-effectiveness and widespread availability have made it a widely applied technique in this field. However, there are some methodological limitations, especially when applied to fine ceramics: its efficiency may be limited in identifying provenance and in studying production technology. However, petrographic analysis of fine ceramics may still provide some valuable information; for example, distinguishing between calcareous and non-calcareous clays. Additionally, it enables a broad estimation of the firing temperature based on the observation of the vitrification grade of the ceramic matrix, thus providing clues about the potential firing temperatures of the sample. This method is also useful for studying slips and glazes as it allows us to observe their internal microstructure and examine the interaction between the glaze and the clay body. It also enables us to identify unfused inclusions and new reaction phases, as well as determine whether pigments are applied over or under the glaze (see Section 6).

Petrographic analysis is inherently destructive; it involves cutting a sufficiently small piece from the sample to create thin sections. In such cases, its application to very small samples or to precious artefacts from museums is limited or not feasible. One further drawback of this method is that it requires specialized knowledge in geology, particularly in the fields of petrology and sedimentology, and hence, requires intensive training.

2.1.2 Scanning Electron Microscopy (SEM) and SEM-EDX

The scanning electron microscope (SEM) is a powerful imaging technique that is widely used for obtaining high-resolution images and detailed information about the surface and near-surface structures of a broad spectrum of solid materials. SEM utilizes a focused beam of electrons to scan the surface of a specimen. This electron beam interacts with the atoms on the surface of the sample, generating signals that can be detected and transformed into high-resolution images (Ul-Hamid 2018).

This is a useful technique applied to studying a wide range of archaeological materials, involving ceramic and inorganic painting decoration of ceramics (Tite 1992; Burnstock & Jones 2000; Froh 2004).

Measurement in an SEM is inherently non-destructive and is generally operated in a vacuum (typically 10–5 mbar). However, as the sample chamber has a limited volume, only small objects, such as arrowheads, coins, or small shards, can primarily be analysed without sample preparation. Alternatively, in a specially designed large sample chamber, non-invasive measurement can also be achieved (Barnes 1991). In the case of analysing a ceramic body (paste), the sample should be prepared, thus making the measurement destructive in this instance. Generally, a polished surface of ceramic is prepared and coated with a thin layer of gold or carbon (typical thickness of 50 nm) prior to the measurements, to prevent the build-up of electric charge on the specimen, when bombarded with electrons (Burnstock & Jones 2000).

There is a wide range of potential applications for analytical SEM in the field of archaeological materials. SEM provides insights into the physical properties and microstructural characterization of both raw materials and finished ceramics. It also contributes to provenance studies; however, its primary use in ceramic studies is the investigation of production technologies, specifically the estimation of firing temperature (Tite 1992). This is achieved through the characterization of the various stages of vitrification, which depend on the firing temperature. The high-resolution SEM images (Figure 1e), typically on the order of 1–2 nanometers, enable the examination of the microstructure of ceramics, allowing for the estimation of the potential or maximum firing temperature of the ceramic (Tite 1992; Froh 2004). Modern SEM is commonly combined with energy-dispersive X-ray analysis (EDX), also known as SEM-EDX. This combination allows for the determination of the elemental composition of selected spots on samples, enabling the identification of specific inclusions in the matrix or areas on the surface, such as different pigments. SEM-EDX also facilitates the identification of elemental variation in a specific surface area on the sample, known as elemental mapping (Froh 2004; Aprile et al. 2019).

Due to its flexibility, especially when combined with EDX (Energy Dispersive X-ray Spectroscopy), this technique is highly versatile. It can operate both as a destructive and non-destructive method, depending on the research question and/or the area to be analysed. This capability makes SEM-EDX a preferred technique for comprehensive material characterization in ceramic archaeometry. SEM analyses are also essential for analysing slips and glazes to observe the microstructure and analyse the slips/glaze themselves (see Section 6).

2.2 Mineralogical Analysis

One of the main objectives of ceramic archaeometric studies is the investigation of the mineralogical characteristics of the ceramic material. The knowledge of the mineral composition of the sample – entire paste, or a part, such as the matrix or specific components of fabric – painting pigments, or slip, provides valuable information on various archaeological questions. Though mineralogical analysis can also reveal information that can be useful in assigning the possible origin of the ceramic raw material, its application, however, usually addresses the questions concerning the manufacturing techniques, such as firing temperature, firing atmosphere, or surface treatment, as well as various decoration techniques like painting. The mineralogy by definition includes the crystalline phase analysis, such as quartz or clay minerals. The methods also involve the determination of the non-crystalline constituents, for example, the amorphous constituents. Depending on the goal of the study, there is a wide range of methods that can be utilized in the examination of the mineralogical composition of ceramic materials, some of which may require sample preparation (destructive methods), and others can be conducted without any sample preparation (non-destructive methods). The choice of the mineralogical methods, as with other techniques, depends on various factors (see also earlier). For example, to determine a detailed mineral composition through powder XRD analysis, a fine-powdered sample material is required, thus making it a destructive method. On the other hand, a surface analysis, for example, painting decoration using Raman spectroscopy or Micro X-ray diffraction, can be performed directly on the surface without sample preparation. Next, the application of powder XRD analysis, one of the preferred methods in archaeological ceramic studies, is briefly presented in relation to ceramic materials.

2.2.1 X-ray Diffraction

X-ray diffraction (XRD) is a well-established and widely used analytical method for determining the mineralogical composition of various inorganic materials, including archaeological ceramics. This method works by irradiating the sample surface with incident X-rays and measuring the intensities and angles of the X-ray reflections, and through Bragg's Law, which explains the relationship between the angles of incidence and the resulting diffraction patterns (for technical details, e.g. Heimann 2017).

XRD analysis on powdered samples (Powder XRD) requires sample preparation and is therefore destructive. A small portion of the sample from a ceramic shard, about 0.2–0.5 g, needs to be fine powdered, usually in an agate mortar, until the particle size is uniform and less than 20 µm. The mineral composition of the powdered sample is then analysed. Based on the generated signals, the mineral phases are identified using the International Centre for Diffraction Data (ICDD) PDF database.

XRD is also widely used to investigate the production processes of ceramics, with particular emphasis on the raw materials used and the firing temperature and atmosphere (Maggetti 1982; Cultrone et al. 2001; Trindade et al. 2009). The method also is useful to examine the possible post-depositional alteration processes of ceramics (Heimann & Maggetti 1981; Schwedt et al. 2006). Another area of its application is the analysis of mineral-based painting decoration of ceramics (Moon et al. 2021).

One of the strengths of this method in ceramics study is that it enables the identification of fine crystalline phases. This is particularly useful for fine ceramics, where petrographic methods provide limited information (see Section 2.1). It allows for the investigation of the mineralogical composition of the clay. In low-fired ceramics, it may also be possible to determine the initial clay minerals of raw clay. XRD is a useful tool, especially in the estimation of the firing temperature of ceramic vessels which is one of the key questions largely subjected in many archaeometric studies, as this provides information to understand the technological procedures applied by the ancient potters. This concept relies on the presence or absence of certain minerals, referred to as indicator minerals, of sample under investigation. Such indicator minerals are for example calcite, hematite, mullite, gehlenite, or diopside. During the firing process, specific chemical reactions occur within the clay paste. Depending on factors such as firing temperature, firing atmosphere, mineralogical composition, and the fineness of the raw clay, some minerals disappear at specific higher temperatures, while others are newly formed. By identifying such indicator minerals, it is possible to determine the firing temperature (or temperature interval) of the ceramic (Gliozzo 2020). Besides its primary application in exploring the production processes of ceramics, XRD analysis, especially of fine ceramics, can also provide valuable information for the interpretation of chemical data. This is particularly relevant in regard to provenance identification.

Due to its easy accessibility in many laboratories, cost-effectiveness, and other advantages, powder XRD is one of the preferred analytical techniques applied in ceramic archaeometric studies. XRD is also used to identify crystalline compounds in glazes. It can be performed directly on the surface of the glaze, provided the surface is sufficiently flat. The depth to which X-rays penetrate the glaze varies depending on its composition, typically ranging from a few micrometres to tens of micrometres. This variability can sometimes limit the identification of compounds near the glaze-ceramic interface. Transmission μ-XRD using synchrotron light offers the advantage of accessing different areas across the thin (50–100 µm) cross section of the glaze with micrometre-level resolution (Pradell & Molera 2020).

2.2.2 Raman Spectroscopy

Among the various analytical techniques used in archaeometric studies for examining mineralogical compositions, Raman spectroscopy has become a significant tool during the last decades for exploring and characterizing a wide range of archaeological materials (Edwards et al. 2023). Raman spectroscopy identifies molecular structures and composition of sample in different states – solids, liquids, and gases – making it a highly versatile instrument. The technique uses monochromatic light, typically a laser as the light source, which interacts with the molecules in the sample, a small part of the light scattered due to the excitation of the molecular vibrations. This scattered light, known as the Raman scattering effect, is characteristic for specific molecules present and their vibrational modes. By analysing the Raman scattering patterns, a fingerprint of the sample's composition can be determined, hence enables the identification of various constituents, the study of their structures, and the quantification of their abundance (e.g., Edwards et al. 2023 for details).

The technique is inherently non-destructive or minimally invasive, as it allows samples to be analysed in their natural state without the need for extensive preparation such as cutting, powdering, or dissolving. However, in the case of laboratory-based analysis, if a sample is too large to fit into the sample compartment, a small portion of sample (c. 1 g) may need to be removed from the larger sample. A notable advantage of Raman spectroscopy, compared to other mineralogical analytical techniques such as X-ray diffraction, is its ability to identify both crystalline and amorphous components, as well as organic-based materials. Furthermore, owing to continuous technological advancements, Raman spectroscopy has further advantages in terms of smaller instrument size and improved transportability, facilitated by better laser sources, electronics, and CCD detectors (Vandenabeele et al. 2007). Its flexibility in application and the analytical performance have contributed to its growing popularity, leading to its widespread application across a vast range of research areas, including archaeometry, art history, conservation and restoration, and many other fields. In archaeometric studies, Raman spectroscopy has been extensively applied to analyse a wide variety of material categories, such as metals, vitreous materials like glass and glazes, pigments, ceramics, biomaterials, and others, to address a different set of research questions (e.g., Edwards et al. 2023).

Concerning the archaeometric analysis of ceramic materials, its previous application has focused more on surface decorations, such as painting pigments and glazes (see Section 6). Especially in the study of paintings, Raman spectroscopy offers some benefits compared to other methods, such as XRD. This technique is able to identify not only mineral-based pigments (inorganic crystalline phases) but also organic-based pigments. This can be particularly important in cases where there is no prior information about the possible pigment types (organic or inorganic origin). Though the application of Raman spectroscopy to the analysis of the ceramic body composition, for example to identify mineral inclusions in ceramics, has been used (e.g., Wopenka et al. 2002; Medeghini et al. 2013), its use for the analysis of the ceramic body is still limited, compared to the study of surface decorations. As this method is capable of identifying the mineralogical phases of ceramics, for example, on a small powder samples or other sampling forms, it can provide valuable information, particularly on the production techniques. This may include identifying mineral phase which were newly formed during the firing process, such as mullite, diopside, wollastonite, or other minerals, as well as amorphous components that may be critical to determining the firing setting of ancient ceramic production.

Identifying the material composition in a sample using Raman spectroscopy is typically based on the comparison of the characteristic vibrational spectra of the sample to reference spectra in a database. For this purpose, there exist freely accessible databases containing reference spectra for a wide range of materials, including minerals, ceramics, pigments, glasses, organic compounds, and other sample types. The most frequently used databases are the RRUFF database (http://rruff.info/) and the IRUG (Infrared and Raman Users Group) database (http://www.irug.org/). There are also several other open-access libraries available (for further details and references, see Edwards et al. 2023: 37–38). When integrated with other commonly used analytical techniques – such as X-ray fluorescence (XRF) and scanning electron microscopy coupled with energy-dispersive X-ray spectroscopy (SEM-EDS) – Raman spectroscopy can provide additional advantages for comprehensive materials characterization, thereby enabling the exploration of a broader spectrum of archaeological research questions.

Raman spectroscopy is today considered as one of the most suitable instrumental techniques. This is mainly due to the sensitivity, high analytical performance, and non-destructive analysis capabilities of the technique, as well as the flexibility of its application for the analysis of diverse material groups. It is to be expected that the continuing development of new, non-invasive instrumentation and the availability of portable and handheld device setups (see Section 2.4.2) will further contribute to its widespread use in archaeometric studies of ceramic materials.

2.3 Chemical Analysis

Chemical analysis deals with the determination of the elemental composition of ceramics. These are the major and minor elements, typically SiO_2, TiO_2, Al_2O_3, Fe_2O_3 (total), MnO, MgO, CaO, Na_2O, K_2O, and P_2O_5. Their concentrations are normally expressed as a weight percent (wt.%) of the oxide and a large number of trace elements (usually 20–40), those elements which are present at less than the 0.1 wt.%, and their concentrations are normally expressed in parts per million (ppm).

The chemical analysis focuses particularly on the provenance identification of ceramic, that is, the place of the raw clay source and/or production place. It can also provide some valuable information about the type of raw material used (e.g., calcareous, non-calcareous clay), the production mode, and other information. Thus, the determination of the chemical composition of ceramics is one of the primary research approaches in ceramic investigation. In the provenance studies, there is a basic concept known as the provenance postulate. This concept, first proposed by Weigand et al. (1977), posits that 'there exist differences in chemical composition between different natural sources that exceed, in some recognizable way, the differences observed within a given source'. To state it differently: Ceramics manufactured from a specific raw clay and using the same paste preparation process display similar elemental composition (similar chemical fingerprint) that can be distinguished from ceramics made from different other clay deposits (e.g., Neff 2000). Although the universal validity of the provenance postulate could not be proven (Hein & Kilikoglou 2020a), numerous studies have shown that this postulate is applicable to the examination of pottery for archaeometric studies.

Achieving a successful archaeological ceramic analysis requires meeting several criteria, with the most significant ones being the discriminative power of a method (analytical performance; precision, accuracy, and lower detection limit of element concentrations), as well as the number of measured elements including major and trace elements (e.g., Tite 2008; Hazenfratz-Marks 2017). There is a wide range of methods available for determining the elemental composition of ceramics and reference samples (Pollard et al. 2007). Next, we outline some of the most important and widely applied methods.

2.3.1 X-Ray Fluorescence Spectrometry

X-ray Spectrometry (XRF) is a well-established analytical technique widely applied in scientific and industrial fields to determine the major, minor, and trace elements composition of various materials, ranging, for example, metals, glasses, ceramics, rocks, pigments, as well as environmental and biological materials and more. The measurement is based on the secondary X-rays emitted by the sample and thereby the detection of characteristic X-rays by a spectrometer that is used to identify the elements present in the sample and calculate their concentrations. There are several spectrometer techniques in various configurations that were developed and applied for various purposes (Beckhoff et al. 2006; Pollard et al. 2007). Depending on the method of the detection system, this technique is usually divided into two main types: energy-dispersive (ED) and wavelength-dispersive (WD) X-ray fluorescence analysis. EDXRF measures the energy and intensity of the secondary X-rays and is more suited for elements with an atomic number (Z) between 20 and 41. WDXRF measures the wavelengths of the secondary X-rays, and can also measure lighter elements from about $Z = 11$ (e.g., Schramm 2012; Hall 2017).

Principally, due to its non-invasive nature, EDXRF is widely used, in particular, different configurations of EDXRF such as Micro-XRF and portable XRF (see Section 2.4.4); both are non-invasive techniques, are widely applied in the analysis of art, museum, and archaeological objects such as ceramic, metal, glass, manuscripts, paintings, icons, and other (Mantler & Schreiner 2000; Donais & George 2018). Both EDXRF and WD-XRF are two analytical techniques that are able to generate high-quality compositional data and provide a low-cost and rapid measurement of the chemical composition of ceramic materials. Although the samples can be analysed by both methods without sample preparation, for example, in the case of small samples that fit into the sample holder, labour-based analysis can especially benefit from sample preparation for high-quality results. This may include simple cleaning and polishing of the sample surface, powdering, and pelletizing with or without a binder (e.g., ceramic materials), fusing the sample with appropriate flux (ceramics, rocks, ores, etc.).

Both laboratory-based ED XRF and WDXRF methods have been successfully used in ceramic research as shown in numerous studies (e.g., Papachristodoulou et al. 2006; Kibaroğlu et al. 2009; 2011). The measured elements show a high precision, largely even comparable with NAA data (Müller et al. 2018). Nevertheless, both spectroscopic methods have advantages and disadvantages when compared. For example, EDXRF is considered a fast method that allows the determination of several elements simultaneously with high accuracy. In addition, EDXRF is also cheaper and more easily accessible. However, WDXRF has its own advantages over EDXRF. Elements with lower Z, such as Na, Mg, P, Al, and Si, are best measured using WDXRF spectrometry (Hall 2017). WDXRF spectrometers can also more readily measure some of the REEs (rare earth elements) that may be significant in provenance identification. WDXRF spectrometers generally have superior detection limits over EDXRF spectrometers (Jenkins 1999; Janssen 2004).

Both spectroscopic techniques are powerful tools for the examination of ceramic materials. As in the case of other analytical techniques, method selection usually depends on several criteria such as research questions, expected results (quantitative or semi-quantitative analysis, determination of element suites), performance, sample size, cost issues, availability of the technique, and others (Hall 2017).

2.3.2 Neutron Activation Analysis

Neutron Activation Analysis (NAA) is a well-established and frequently employed analytical technique for determining the elemental composition of various materials, including archaeological ceramic materials (Perlman & Asaro 1969; Harbottle 1976; Glascock 1992). This is a nuclear analytical technique that uses the emission of characteristic gamma rays from a sample that has been irradiated with neutrons to determine the concentration of elements in the sample (Neff 2000; Glascock & Neff 2003).

For the measurement of elemental composition, relatively little effort is generally required for sample preparation. The sample can be removed by breaking off a small piece of the sherd and then grinding it, or by scraping, drilling, or burring it from the material. The prepared sample, commonly in the form of powder, is placed on a gamma ray detector and then irradiated. The required sample size depends on the homogeneity of the sherd. For inhomogeneous samples, for example, coarse ceramics, more material may be needed. Although NAA can also measure very small samples (30 mg), there may be some loss of precision in the case of such small sizes. Therefore, for an adequate measurement, a sample size of between 100 and 150 mg is typically needed (Neff 2000; Sterba 2018).

NAA has a number of advantages over most other analytical methods, especially in regard to archaeological materials such as ceramic provenance studies. NAA is capable of measurements of a large range of major, minor, and trace elements with high precision, accuracy, and sensitivity, which may be important for reliable provenance identification. This is a significant advantage for archaeological studies, as it allows the analysis of small size or valuable artefacts, without leaving remarkable traces. A further advantage is that measurement is nearly free of any matrix interference effects. The comparability of NAA data from different laboratories is possible without major conversions, so existing databases can be used as a reference group for provenance studies (Neff 2000). This is especially beneficial for ceramic research, where there is a large NAA database available (ceraDAT[1], MURR[2]).

NAA is a cost-intensive technique, though its expenses can vary depending on several factors, including reactor costs, equipment expenses, reference

---

[1] https://ceradat.net/   [2] https://archaeometry.missouri.edu/murr_database.html

materials, the number of samples, and overall labour costs. One of the main disadvantages of NAA is that it can only be performed in a research reactor. Due to the limited availability of such reactors, only a few research groups at well-funded government laboratories have been able to explore new applications for nuclear techniques. As a result, there are only a limited number of laboratories around the world that perform NAA; notable examples are the Missouri University Research Reactor (MURR) and TU Wien Atominstitut, Austria. This has led to a kind of monopoly, with research dependencies on these few laboratories. A significant problem is also nuclear waste disposal. Though there are relatively small amounts of radioactive waste produced, its disposal is challenging. As Neff (2000) forecasted 20 years ago, as a result of environmental concerns related to nuclear waste and the construction of new reactors, a declining trend in the use of NAA can be observed, and this method is increasingly being replaced by other methods, such as Laser Ablation Inductively Coupled Plasma Mass Spectrometry (ICP-MS).

2.3.3 Inductively Coupled Plasma Mass Spectrometry

ICP-MS (inductively coupled plasma mass spectrometry) is a powerful analytical technique, widely employed in diverse research fields including geoscience, archaeological science, and industrial sectors. Due to its ability to perform rapid multi-element determinations at the ultra-trace level and technical improvements in instrumentation, ICP-MS has been one of the fastest-growing analytical techniques in recent years. The basic principle of measurement is to ionize atoms using suitable ionization methods, separate the ions by their mass-to-charge ratio (m/z), and then record the mass spectrum using a recording device (e.g., Pollard et al. 2007; Thomas 2013).

Although the first ICP-MS was introduced in the early 1980s, and was subsequently applied in various fields, such as in geology, its application in ceramic archaeometry has become increasingly popular, especially in the recent decade (e.g., Giussani et al. 2009; Resano et al. 2010; Golitko & Dussubieux 2017; Kibaroğlu et al. 2019; Williams et al. 2023). There are two main types of ICP-MS instruments mostly used in ceramic archaeometry: Digestion (or Solution) ICP-MS and Laser Ablation-ICP-MS. Both methods have their own applications and advantages in the context of ceramic analysis.

The Digestion-ICP-MS requires the sample to be in a liquid form; therefore, for measurement of solid samples, for example, ceramic, a small part of the sample, typically 100 mg is dissolved in a strong acid, such as nitric acid or hydrochloric acid, generally using microwave technique to obtain an accurate bulk chemical composition of the material (Kennett et al. 2002). Although the

Digestion ICP-MS is a highly sensitive method and needs a small sample size (~100 mg) for measuring the major, minor, and all geochemically relevant trace elements (>40), which offers an advantage in the ceramic provenance study compared to other methods, for example, NAA, however, its wider application in ceramic archaeometry is limited. This is especially due to the health risks associated with acid treatment of the samples and waste disposal, also a time-consuming sample preparation (Little et al. 2004).

Laser Ablation (LA) ICP-MS: Combined with a laser-based sampling system, called Laser Ablation (LA), ICP-MS has become increasingly the most extensively used high-resolution analytical technique for multi-element characterization for a wide variety of archaeological materials such as vitreous materials, ceramics, pigments, metals, human remains, and other archaeomaterials (Giussani et al. 2009; Resano et al. 2010; Dussubieux et al. 2016). The use of LA-ICP-MS in ceramic archaeometry has increased in recent years rapidly, due to technological development and the resulting improvement in analytical performance (Speakman & Neff 2002; Golitko & Dussubieux 2017; Kibaroğlu et al. 2019; Williams et al. 2023).

The ablated sample from the ablation cell is first transported into the plasma torch by argon or helium gas. The produced aerosol is then ionized in the plasma, passing through the mass spectrometer where the ions are measured by a detector (Giussani et al. 2009; Thomas 2013 for further details). LA-ICP-MS has a number of advantages over other analytical techniques that make it the method of choice for various fields of archaeological science. Some important advantages of this method, among others within the ceramic examination, are its capability to identify a large number of elements (>40), including major, minor, and trace elements (including Rare Earth Element-REEs), with high analytical performance, which are important criteria for a reliable provenance identification. Major elements can also be identified without external measurement, using the normalization technique (Gratuze et al. 2001).

The surface damage caused by the laser ablation is minimal, in most cases invisible to the naked eye, having a typical diameter of 50–200 μm. Small sherd samples, fitting into the ablation cell, can also be analysed directly, on a cleaned specific surface (typically clay matrix) without sample preparation (e.g., Eckert & James 2011; Sharratt et al. 2015; Shoval 2017). In this way, however, the measured element composition is a 'pseudo-bulk' composition. To address this, and to obtain bulk chemical data that is representative of the sample, the measurement needs to be performed on press-pellet (6–8 mm in diameter) that is perpetrated from 0.5 to 1.0 g homogenized ultra-fine sample powders (Kibaroğlu et al. 2019). As the LA-ICP-MS has micrometre spatial resolution (50–100 μm), it is also possible to analyse particular mineral inclusions (Gehres

& Querré 2018) or components included in a ceramic sample. A notable drawback is up to today the limitation of matrix-matched Standard Reference Materials (RMS) for quantitative analyses of archaeological ceramics.

The increasing availability of LA-ICP-MS in numerous laboratories, combined with technological advancements, makes this method appealing for various research areas. The portable laser ablation techniques for sampling (pLA-ICP-MS), a new development (see Section 2.4.5), provide new opportunities in the archaeometry research area.

2.4 Portable Methods

In applying analytical methods to historic materials – such as museum objects or archaeological artefacts – a general concern is preserving the integrity of the object. Particularly in the case of precious and unique objects, the application of destructive methods is principally not available. On the other hand, from an analytical/scientific perspective, it is crucial to determine the mineralogical and/or chemical characteristics of the object under study as precisely as possible. Consequently, a primary objective for archaeometry is to continually evolve new tools that meet this requirement. For many years various portable geochemical, mineralogical, and optical methods have been applied to archaeological pottery either in the field or in the laboratory. Due to their compact design and the technical adaptations required, these methods are often less sensitive than their laboratory counterparts, but their great advantage is that they can be used directly in museums or on excavations. This makes it possible to analyse samples that cannot be transported, either because of their size or because of export restrictions, and also to collaborate with specialists in order to optimize the sampling procedure and thus the results. Comparably short measurement times and immediate results make portable methods a valuable, time, and cost-effective tool (Potts 2008; Nakai & Abe 2012; Frahm & Doonan 2013; Jehlička & Culka 2022).

When choosing a portable method, the first thing to decide is whether it should be a mobile or handheld option. While the former are benchtop systems, which are often heavy and sometimes require additional equipment such as transformers, special sample holders, and sample preparation equipment, handheld instruments are easy to transport and can be used directly on the sample in almost all conditions. Mobile instruments require a stationary field laboratory with a stable power source, whereas handheld instruments can run on batteries alone and, as the name suggests, can be held in the hand and therefore also applied in situ (Potts 2008; Frahm & Doonan 2013; Vandenabeele & Donais 2016; Jehlička & Culka 2022).

Portable systems are available for mineralogical analysis such as X-ray diffraction (p-XRD) or Raman spectroscopy (p-RS), but also for chemical analysis including X-ray fluorescence (p-XRF), Fourier transform infrared spectroscopy (p-FTIR) and laser-induced breakdown spectroscopy (p-LIBS), to name just a view. While p-XRD is best suited to determine raw materials and pottery manufacturing techniques, such as firing temperatures and clay types, from their mineral composition, p-RS provides information on the (in)organic components present, helping to identify pigments and organic residues, as well as crystalline phases and structural features. p-FTIR helps to define functional groups and molecules, enabling the detection of organic residues, surface treatments, and changes due to external factors. To determine the chemical composition using non-destructive methods, several techniques have already been adopted: p-XRF characterizes an elemental fingerprint to understand sourcing and production patterns, trade networks, and cultural links based on geographical origin and the presence of specific trace elements. A promising new analytical technique in this context is portable laser ablation inductively coupled plasma mass spectrometry (pLA-ICP-MS), which is capable of not only analysing the chemical composition but also controlling the depth of analysis which is important, for example, for glazes.

2.4.1 Portable X-ray Diffraction Analysis (p-XRD)

Portable mobile XRD and laboratory XRD are both used to determine the crystal structure of materials (see Section 2.2.1). However, while the latter offers greater precision and detailed analysis, the former has the advantage of portability and rapid on-site analysis, making it a valuable tool for field work and in situ characterization of materials. However, measurements can take up to 60 minutes due to the limited size of the portable instruments and the resulting need to adjust the placement of components in a slightly less-optimal way. Also the detection limit is quite low, allowing mainly the major phases to be investigated. p-XRD instruments are available from a number of manufacturers and differ in aspects such as measurement mode, calibration, data processing, and overall performance. Additionally, measurement spot size, arrangement of components, and the mounting of the device itself can be adjusted. It is therefore important to be well informed about which application is best suited to the user's purpose, which will require a certain investment of time in research and training for the user to achieve reliable and useful results. Laboratory XRD typically requires extensive sample preparation including grinding and homogenization to ensure uniformity and accurate results. In contrast, portable XRD requires less sample preparation for polycrystalline materials such as ceramics, often limited to cleaning the surface to remove contaminants. This makes it suitable for objects that are too valuable to allow even a small area of the surface to be removed. However, this means that any surface contamination will inevitably affect the analysis results. In terms of handling, the sample must be placed in a fixed distance in the centre of the goniometric circle, the latter being the part of the apparatus that controls the exact angular position of the sample relative to the beam and the detector. Generally speaking, only one measurement per sample is taken (Pappalardo et al. 2008; Romano et al. 2011; Nakai & Abe 2012).

2.4.2 Portable Raman Spectroscopy (p-RS)

Raman spectroscopy (see Section 2.2.2) is used to identify mineral phases in archaeological pottery, with the ability to analyse amorphous materials such as carbon. While laboratory RS instruments are typically large and stationary, requiring a controlled laboratory environment, portable RS instruments are compact, mobile or handheld, allowing easy transport and operation in different locations, including the field or remote environments. The latter are well suited for rapid on-site analysis without the need for complex sample preparation procedures, as surface cleaning is sufficient, while the former offer higher precision and detailed analysis. While mobile instruments can be used flexibly because the probe can be positioned independently of the rest of the necessary equipment, handheld instruments are more suitable for field work. The technology uses a laser to induce Raman scattering, the spectrum of which can be used to identify the molecule in the sample by comparing the visible spectrum with a reference database. A measurement can take between 5 and 30 minutes, depending on the instrument and setup. Some studies used very short measurement times of only 20 seconds with three measurements per sample, holding the instrument at a distance corresponding to the focal point of the instrument. It is worth mentioning that the method is not fully suitable for quantitative analysis and the spectra can be difficult to interpret. In addition, mobile instruments need to be mounted in a stable position, with the ability to move around the sample. As with all methods, it is important to be aware of the specifics of the instrument – in this case, excitation wavelength, fibre availability, and so on. It is also very important to get familiar with the standards of the method and to follow a strict protocol for sampling and data processing. Even if the method is normally non-destructive, it may be minimally invasive if the laser power is too high for the sample. Therefore, sample properties and laser energy must be carefully monitored to avoid destroying parts of the sample (Nakai & Abe 2012; Vandenabeele & Donais 2016; Barone et al. 2017; Jehlička & Culka 2022).

2.4.3 Portable Fourier Transform Infrared Spectroscopy (p-FTIR)

Portable Fourier Transform Infrared Spectroscopy is used mainly for the study of painted pottery, aiding in the identification of ceramic bodies, glazes, pigments, and firing temperatures. To identify the mineralogical composition not only of crystalline but also of pseudo-amorphous thermal phases, infrared spectroscopy uses a broad spectrum of infrared light to excite the molecules in a sample that absorb the infrared radiation. They begin to vibrate in characteristic ways which are processed, and the interference patterns are analysed and converted into a spectrum by a mathematical transformation (= Fourier transformation). This then provides information about the functional groups and chemical components in the sample, as the visible peaks correspond to the specific molecular vibrations. The mid-infrared range is often applied for excitation, but if molecules with functional groups such as N-H, O-H, or C-H are to be identified, the near-infrared range should also be used. As this method is non-destructive, it is also susceptible to surface contamination and curvature. The measurement time can vary (4 to 8 minutes) with a measurement spot size of approximately 0.6 cm and a collection of at least one spectrum per sample. Again, an in-depth knowledge of measurement parameters and data processing is required to obtain reliable results. Spectra can be improved by using powder samples. This reduces external reflection and improves the signal-to-noise ratio. Knowledge of data processing and interpretation of peaks for identification of composition phases by using literature or reference materials is essential to achieve high-quality research results (Bruni et al. 2023).

2.4.4 Portable X-ray Fluorescence Analysis (p-XRF)

Like their laboratory counterparts, mobile and handheld X-ray fluorescence analysers (Figure 2) can be used to determine the chemical composition of pottery samples in the field. This allows the identification of elements present in the pottery, providing information on raw materials and possibly their origin. Therefore, p-XRF can help answer key research questions such as the provenance of pottery, trade and exchange networks, technological advancements, and cultural interactions. However, due to its limited range of detectable elements but short measurement time, this method is often used as a preliminary screening tool or complementary method. While laboratory (see Section 2.3.1) and mobile XRF analysis provide high accuracy and detailed elemental information, they also require samples to be transported to a laboratory involving more extensive sample preparation. On the other hand, handheld p-XRF analysis offers rapid on-site analysis with minimal sample preparation preserving the integrity of valuable artefacts and providing immediate data that can inform

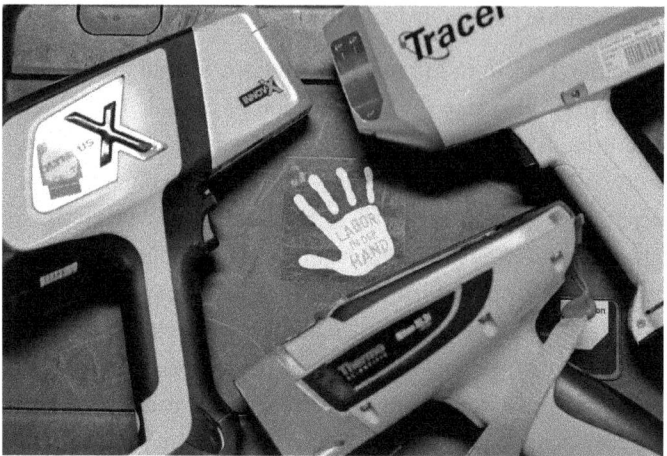

Figure 2 A variety of producers offer handheld p-XRF devices, © M. Schauer

ongoing archaeological investigations. Measurement time can – due to application and device – vary between about 6 minutes and 10 seconds. These instruments are available from a variety of manufacturers, each providing their own measurement settings (methods) and data processing algorithms. It is therefore necessary to understand the specific instrument in sufficient detail to be able to select the appropriate measurement parameters and apply the best method of data quality control and processing. While understanding these details can be tricky, the practical operation of the instruments is quite simple: equipped with a simple trigger, the nose of the instrument must be as close to the sample as possible. The surface to be analysed should be as smooth and free of contamination as possible. For this reason, fresh brakes are often produced to allow at least three non-overlapping measurements per sample. However, as with p-XRD, handheld p-XRF can be used in a completely non-destructive manner with the same implications for data interpretation (Potts 2008; Frahm & Doonan 2013; Shugar & Mass 2014; Vandenabeele & Donais 2016).

2.4.5 Portable Laser Ablation Inductively Coupled Plasma Mass Spectrometry

The portable laser ablation ICP-MS technique is a combination of two different instrumentations that work in different settings. The main difference in this method compared to the standard LA-ICP-MS (Section 2.3.3) is the sampling technique. While in a lab-based setup, a stationary ablation device with a sample chamber of limited size is used, pLA-ICP-MS uses a specifically designed portable laser ablation sampling device, which allows in situ sampling of arbitrarily sized objects in the field and museum setting (Glaus et al. 2012; Knaf et al. 2017). The prime component is the portable LA sampling device, which basically consists of a pulsed laser, an optical fibre attached to a hand-held LA module, a sampling filter mounting, and a membrane pump. For sampling, the LA module is applied to the sample surface, and the produced particles, as aerosol particles, are collected on membrane filters with sub-micrometre pore size. After the on-site sampling procedure, the filters are re-ablated using a standard laser device used in the laboratory with standard settings, the sample is introduced to the mass spectrometer, and the detected element concentrations are measured. Alternatively, from the filter-sampled material, the sample solution is prepared, and subsequent elemental analyses performed with standard ICP-MS (Numrich et al. 2023). An experimental study has presented that quantification of major, minor, and trace elements by means of pLA-ICP-MS is of similar performance as a standard LA-ICP-MS setup. Compared to other portable techniques, such as X-ray fluorescence spectroscopy (XRF), multiple orders of magnitude lower limits of detection can be obtained (Glaus et al. 2012). The pLA-ICP-MS technique has already been successfully applied to different archaeological materials, including metals (copper, silver, gold, e.g. Burger et al. 2017; Seman et al. 2020), jade, and porcelain (Käser 2015). Experimental analysis by Glaus et al. (2012) also demonstrated the suitability of this method for archaeological ceramic materials.

The pLA-ICP-MS opens a novel possibility in the archaeometric analysis of cultural-historical objects, which for various reasons cannot be analysed destructively. Regarding ceramic analysis, its application is still in the initial phase, but it also offers opportunities to analyse the ceramic body itself and also surface decorations (painting and glaze) with high sensitivity. A drawback of this method is its limited availability, as currently there are only four sampling devices available (Knaf et al. 2017). However, it can be presumed that with the further development of this technique, both internally and in its device components, there will be an increasing popularity.

3 Material Testing of Pottery

Anno Hein

The different functions of the vessels, such as storage, cooking, processing, or transport, required different mechanical and thermal performance of the base material. For storage or transport vessels, for example, mechanical strength and toughness are the main criteria, while porosity became important when liquids were stored or transferred as they required sufficient impermeability of the ceramic walls. A basic difference between storage and transport vessels might have been their total weight, depending on material density, wall thickness, and size. While a transport vessel including its content was supposed to be lifted and moved, the mechanical strength of a storage vessel could be enhanced, for example, by thickening its walls, regardless of its final weight. Thermal properties, such as thermal conductivity, heat capacity, or thermal expansion, were rather relevant for vessels used for processing materials or substances by applying heat. Cooking pots, which were placed directly on or over a fire, differed in terms of design and performance from cooking pots placed in an oven, which were potentially even closed with a lid. Due to their basic refractoriness ceramic vessels could also be used at substantially higher temperatures, such as furnaces or crucibles suitable for metallurgical processing or glass making.

In the present section the thermomechanical properties of ceramic materials will be discussed in view of the performance of functional ceramic vessels designed and used for specific purposes, in which they were exposed to thermal and/or mechanical loads. Approaches towards investigating technical choices made by the craftspeople for the manufacture of ceramics will be exemplified as well as diagnostic techniques for measuring specific physical properties.

3.1 Ceramics as Functional Materials

Ceramics as a material category are defined as inorganic and non-metallic materials, comprising clay minerals, high-temperature phases and non-plastic accessory minerals, with a prevalently polycrystalline microstructure and with the exception of quartz inclusions ionic bonding. Apart from crystalline phases, the ceramic body potentially can also contain amorphous phases, such as organic components or glassy phases, the extent of which essentially depends on the initial firing conditions. Ceramics can be classified as brittle materials showing primarily elastic deformation under external stress but at the same time high stiffness of the ceramic body. They exhibit comparably high hardness and compressive strength, while the tensile strength is usually lower. Pure and independent tensile stress, though, is rather not expected during typical use of, for example, a ceramic vessel. Critical loads have to be considered commonly in the case of bending or flexure, in which a component of the stress tensor might exceed the tensile strength, resulting in crack initiation and ultimate failure of the ceramic structure. The strength of the ceramic material and the Young's modulus, which is a measure of its stiffness, are substantially related to the density of the ceramic body, which depends on its components and on its pore structure. Also the crack development and the fracture mode depend essentially on the ceramics' microstructure. In a pure brittle fracture, typically in the case of a fine and high-fired ceramic fabric, unstable crack propagation emerges after the yield strength is exceeded and the ceramic body will fail instantaneously. In a stable or quasi stable fracture, on the other hand, the fracture energy up to some extent is absorbed in the ceramic body through deflection of the crack propagation by non-plastic inclusions even after the initial failure. The material toughness describes the entire intrinsic fracture energy absorbed by the ceramic body during crack initiation and crack propagation (Kilikoglou et al. 1998; Müller et al. 2010). In contrast to the performance under slow and constant stress the impact resistance of the ceramic body describes the energy absorption during instant and rapid loading, such as the result of dropping or being hit, which might be the most critical damage scenario after all (Bronitsky & Hamer 1986; Tite et al. 2002).

Concerning thermal performance ceramic materials exhibit, first of all, a considerable heat resistance. They remain stable in terms of microstructure and composition at comparably high temperatures, which can typically reach at least up to their initial firing temperature. Their specific heat capacity is comparably high while their thermal conductivity remains at a moderate level compared, for example, to materials with metallic bonding. Thus, the heat transfer within a ceramic structure is slower in comparison to a metallic structure and a ceramic object once heated up can effectively store heat energy. Both properties are affected largely by the ceramics' microstructure and particularly its porosity and pore structure. A potential damage risk of ceramics used at high temperatures is the thermal expansion of the ceramic body and its components, which might cause local mechanical stresses potentially exceeding the ceramics' tensile strength. This applies particularly to non-uniform heating of the ceramic body or to elevated thermal expansion of inclusions with the potential to disrupt the ceramic body. Abrupt temperature changes or thermal shock, such as in cases when a cold cooking pot is set directly on a fire or hot food stuff in a heated ceramic pan is deglazed with a cold fluid, constitute certainly the most critical damage risk due to thermal expansion by inducing extreme temperature gradients (Tite et al. 2002).

3.2 Material Properties and *chaîne opératoire*

Physical properties of ceramics are related to their composition and to their microstructure and, hence, effectively the result of the workflow during the manufacturing process, the so-called *chaîne opératoire*. The performance of the final product can be controlled and adapted to the intended function by the craftsperson through technological choices concerning individual production parameters (Tite et al. 2002; Tite 2008; Roux 2017). Apart from the intrinsic material properties, shape factors and design of the manufactured ceramic vessel have to be considered in view of its performance during the intended use. In the following section the particular steps of the *chaîne opératoire* will be discussed and analytical methods for investigating and assessing technological choices will be introduced.

3.2.1 Raw Material Selection

The first step in the *chaîne opératoire* is the selection of appropriate clayey raw materials (Gualteri 2020). These are commonly collected from raw material deposits in the vicinity of the pottery workshop (Arnold 1985). The collected clayey raw materials can be generally categorized as fine-grained sedimentary rock, in which the actual clay fraction commonly constitutes only one part. The clay fraction is defined by grain size (< 2 µm) and prevalent argillaceous particles with platy crystal structure. Apart from these so-called phyllosilicates, which are predominant in the clay fraction, the raw materials contain typically non-plastic accessory minerals with larger grain sizes. Furthermore, it can contain associated non-crystalline phases, such as organic matter (Bergaya & Lagaly 2006).

When sufficiently high temperatures are reached during firing, the phyllosilicates decompose and new high-temperature mineral phases are formed. The initial clay paste composition, particularly in terms of type and amount of clay minerals, affect the mineralogical composition of the final ceramic product and thus up to a considerable extent the physical properties of the ceramic body. Mineralogical examination of the ceramic body, for example by X-ray Powder Diffraction (XRPD), provides information about the remaining content of phyllosilicate crystals as well as the content of high-temperature crystalline phases formed during firing (Section 2.2; Montana 2020). In combination with elemental analysis this allows for determining the type of raw materials and particularly phyllosilicates, such as illites, serpentines, or kaolinites, which had been selected initially for the manufacture of the ceramics under study (Hein & Kilikoglou 2020a).

3.2.2 Clay Paste Preparation

Depending on the granular composition of the raw materials they have to be processed more or less extensively in order to obtain a workable clay paste (Gosselain & Livingstone Smith 2005). For this, they are commonly first crushed or ground and occasionally sieved in order to remove large non-plastic components. The clay can be furthermore refined by suspending and levigating it in water. Afterwards the refined and homogenized clay paste potentially can be tempered with a controlled amount and size distribution of non-plastic components. Even though in the past the use of diverse temper materials has been occasionally ascribed to cultural factors the temper selection in fact appears to be rather related to the vessel function (Bronitsky & Hamer 1986). After all, temper materials affect the mechanical performance (Kilikoglou et al. 1998; Müller et al. 2015; Allegretta et al. 2015) as well as thermal performance (Hein et al. 2008; Allegretta et al. 2014) of the ceramic material. Aside from tempering, another option for controlling the workability of the clay paste and the physical properties of the final product is the mixing of two or more clayey raw materials from different sources, thus combining different types of phyllosilicates (Betina 2019). Eventually, the clay paste can be mixed also with organic materials, which combust during the firing process. Tempering with organic materials was commonly applied in order to generate additional porosity, which might be advantageous for specific intended functions requiring, for example, thermal shock resistance or the suppression of heat transfer for example in furnace structures (Skibo et al. 1989; Hein et al. 2013). The microstructure of the ceramic body can be investigated with thin-section petrography (see Section 2.1.1). Here, non-plastic inclusions can be identified and assessed in view of natural components or intentional temper, providing information about provenance as well as clay paste processing (Quinn 2022).

3.2.3 Vessel Forming

The next stage in the *chaîne opératoire* is transforming a lump of the processed clay paste into an object with a specific shape, such as a vessel. A decisive technological development in vessel forming was the introduction of a turning base allowing for controlling the rotational symmetry of the vessel during fashioning. The fast turning potter's wheel, eventually, allowed for fashioning the clay by applying rotary kinetic energy (RKE) (Roux 2017; 2019; Thér 2020). Nevertheless, there are numerous forming techniques without using RKE, which are still practiced nowadays. A vessel can be built, for example, by assembling coils or slabs or the clay paste can be pressed or casted into a mould. Eventually, the forming technique affects the distribution and orientation of inclusions and voids in the clay body and in the fired ceramic body accordingly as well as its compaction and density. In consequence, it affects the thermomechanical performance of the ceramic body. The initial forming technique can be investigated by surface examination or by optical microscopy (OM) of the microfabric of the ceramic body (Courty & Roux 1995; Choleva 2012; Thér 2016). The ceramics can be examined non-invasively with X-ray radiography in order to examine their microstructure in view of forming techniques, which, though, still provides only two-dimensional information (Berg 2008; Sanger 2016). Full three-dimensional information of the microstructure can be generated by micro X-ray computer tomography (μCT) (Kozatsas et al. 2018; Gait et al. 2022).

Apart from the intrinsic properties of the ceramic material, though, the vessel performance is affected by its design as well. In this regard design parameters, for example, height, width, wall thickness, and curvature, affect the extensive properties of the vessel, such as weight, volume, stiffness, or heat capacity. The vessel design is decisive for performance and potential damage risk taking into account surface areas presumably exposed to thermomechanical loads, which depend on intended use and application. It can be conventionally examined by measuring the dimensions and generating scaled drawings or taking scaled photographs. In order to generate a digital 3D model this can be complemented by laser-aided profile measurements (Demján et al. 2023) or 3D scanning through photogrammetry, laser scanning, or structured light scanning (Karasik & Smilansky 2008). In the case of closed vessels, though, it is not possible to retrieve full information about wall thickness by 3D scanning. In this case X-ray radiography or X-ray computer tomography can be applied (Berg 2008; Karl et al. 2014).

4 The Firing

Anno Hein

The final step in the *chaîne opératoire* is the firing of the clay body, during which the actual material properties are substantially modified. During the firing process the dried plastic clay body is transformed into a solidified and brittle ceramic body exhibiting resistance against water as well as against mechanical and thermal loads. Material properties of a ceramic object are substantially affected by the temperature regime to which it is exposed during the firing process (Velde & Druc 1999).

At the beginning of the firing process, with increasing temperature first organic matter potentially present in the clay body is combusted and the interlayer water between the clay minerals is completely volatilized. At the further ramp rise of temperature the clay minerals as well as the accessory minerals are decomposed and transformed concomitant with the sintering and vitrification of the microstructure. The phase development of individual components in relation to kiln temperature and atmosphere depends fundamentally on the composition of the clay body and on the granulometry of the different phases (Gliozzo 2020). Basic differences can be observed taking into account, for example, the decomposition of calcite into lime and carbon dioxide at temperatures above 800°C, the dehydroxylation of clay minerals by release of the molecular bonded hydroxyls (OH). Their crystal structure is either modified or eventually completely dissolved and the initially plastic clay body, thus, loses its plasticity. The development of vitrified amorphous or glassy phases, which connect the polycrystalline particles in the ceramic body, affects its elasticity and strength as well as its thermal conductivity (Figure 3).

For this, the investigation of firing conditions allows for assessing and categorizing the ceramics under study in view of potential function and performance. The bulk analysis of the mineralogical composition with XRPD allows for estimating the peak temperature of the firing process based on non-decomposed phyllosilicates and high-temperature phases formed. The amount of amorphous phases can be estimated based on the spectral background of the XRPD analysis (Maritan et al. 2015).

Another common approach for estimating the firing conditions is the direct investigation of glassy phases and the categorization of the degree of vitrification under the scanning electron microscope (SEM) (Figure 4) (Tite & Maniatis 1975; Amicone et al. 2020).

The assessment of the firing conditions can be complemented with differential thermal analysis (DTA) and thermogravimetry (TG), which provide information

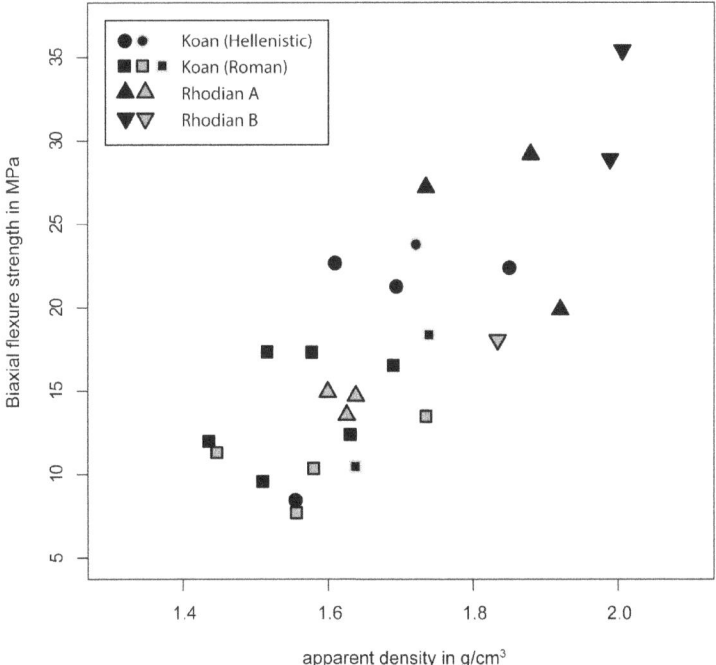

Figure 3 Biaxial flexural strength versus apparent density of Hellenistic and Roman amphora fragments: The symbols indicate the different groups of amphorae. Black symbols indicate extensive or continuous vitrification and grey symbols initial vitrification. The three imported Koan amphorae are indicated with light grey edge lines (Hein et al. 2022).

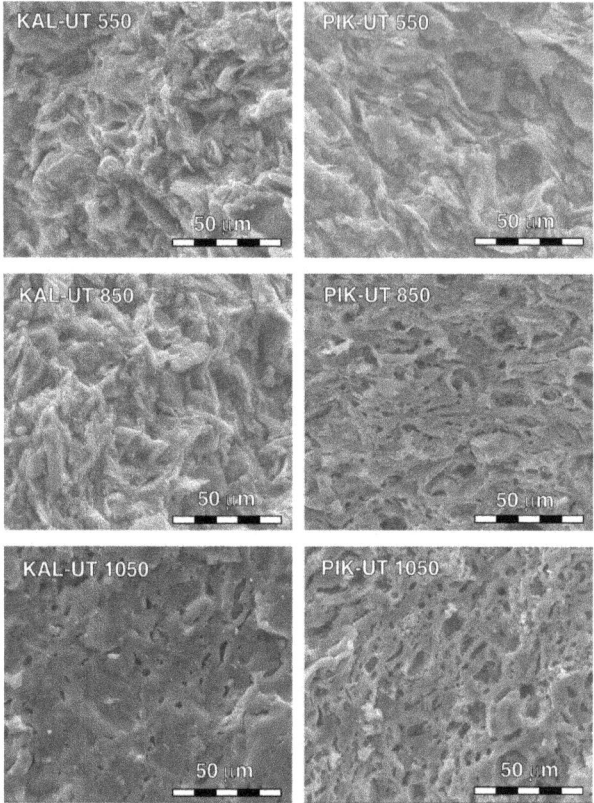

Figure 4 SEM photomicrographs presenting the degree of vitrification observed in specimens of a non-calcareous clay (left) and in a calcareous clay (right) fired at 550°C, 850°C and 1050°C (Hein et al. 2008).

on the temperature range within 250°C and 1100°C (Rice 1987; Moropoulou et al. 1995). These methods are based on the assumption that exothermic reactions of the ceramics emerge at temperatures above the initial firing temperatures (Shoval et al. 1991; Drebushchak et al. 2007). Based on the completion of the dehydroxylation of the present clay minerals, the firing duration can be assessed (Podoba et al. 2012). Eventually, thermoluminescence (TL) provides information about the firing conditions as well, which will be discussed in Section 5.

4.1 Investigation of Thermomechanical Performance

4.1.1 Testing of Thermomechanical Properties

The thermal and/or mechanical performance of ceramic materials in view of their intrinsic material properties can be investigated with material testing according to international standards. For these tests commonly small series of standard shaped specimens, typically bars, disks, or cylinders, of each ceramic material under question have to be prepared. The actual testing, though, often implicates the destruction of the ceramic specimen. Thus, instead of specimens cut and prepared from original archaeological pottery alternatively laboratory specimens can be manufactured and tested replicating specific ceramic fabrics taking into account studies of potential raw materials, observed temper materials and estimated firing conditions. Another advantage of replicates concerns potential alteration or pre-existing flaws in archaeological fragments, which might impair their initial thermomechanical performance.

Since material properties depend up to a large extent on the density or porosity of the material, these parameters should be determined as well. The apparent density can be simply determined by dividing the dry mass of a standard shaped specimen by its volume. The pore size distribution and total porosity can be estimated based on micrographs or µCT scans, or it can be measured by mercury porosimetry (Hein et al. 2013).

Strength

The compressive strength of ceramics can be measured straightforwardly on a test specimen by applying compression along the symmetry axis (Kilikoglou et al. 1998). Compressive strength, though, is rather important for ceramics used as construction materials, such as mudbricks or fired bricks (Özkaya & Böke 2009). In the case of ceramic vessels, it is of minor interest, because pottery vessels are rarely subjected to pure compression during use and they are expected to fail rather due to tensile stresses emerging as components of the stress tensor in bending (Müller et al. 2010). For this, the fracture strength of ceramics is commonly tested in flexure tests, either uni-axial, testing a bar-shaped ceramic specimen in three-point-bending (Kilikoglou et al. 1998; Müller et al. 2010; 2015), or bi-axial, testing a disk-shaped ceramic specimen placed on a hollow steel cylinder with a point load in the centre of the top surface (Hein et al. 2022). The resulting transverse rupture strength (TRS) allows for estimating the tensile strength. It has to be taken into account, though, that it might be affected by pre-existing flaws or other stress concentrators in the tested specimen (Kilikoglou et al. 1998). For this, tests of multiple samples from a specific ceramic fabric are advisable. Alternatively, the tensile strength can be assessed by measuring the Hertzian strength through a spherical load on top of a ceramic disk placed on a plane support surface (Vekinis & Kilikoglou 1998).

Elasticity

The elasticity or Young's modulus can be estimated based on the relation of load and deformation in the curves recorded in the compression or flexure tests

(Kilikoglou et al. 1998; Müller et al. 2010). Due to local collapse of the ceramic matrix under compression, though, potential plastic deformation and an underestimation of the elasticity have to be considered (Hein et al. 2022). Alternatively, elasticity can be determined in dynamic tests using the impulse excitation technique measuring resonance frequencies of flexural vibrations in bar-shaped or disk-shaped specimens (Rambaldi et al. 2017).

Toughness

The toughness of ceramics corresponds to the total fracture energy dissipated in the ceramic body until final failure. During brittle fracture and unstable crack propagation the ceramic body will fail instantaneously after initial crack occurrence. In the case of stable crack propagation additional energy is dissipated until final failure, for example, through inclusions deflecting and impeding the crack propagation (Kilikoglou et al. 1998).

Impact Resistance

The energy dissipation under impact is usually lower than the energy dissipation or toughness under slow constant loading (Tite et al. 2002). The impact resistance of ceramics can be measured, for example, with a weight dropped on a test specimen from a specific height (Skibo et al. 1989) or with a pendulum tester hitting the ceramic specimen with a predefined energy (Bronitsky & Hamer 1986; Müller et al. 2016).

Heat Transfer

The static heat transfer in ceramics can be measured, for example, with a modified Lee's disk setup (Hein et al. 2008, 2013). For this, a disk-shaped ceramic specimen is placed on a heating plate with predefined temperature. A metallic disk with high conductivity is placed on top, and its temperature is recorded until equilibrium of the temperature difference is reached. The temperature-dependent heat loss of the upper disk into the environment provides an estimation of the heat flux and thus allows for determining the thermal conductivity of the sample disk. The transient plane source technique allows for determining the thermal diffusivity and thus, apart from thermal conductivity, also heat capacity (Log & Gustafsson 1995).

Thermal Shock

The thermal expansion of ceramics, which is the source of failure under thermal shock, can be measured by heating bar-shaped or cylindrical specimens and by measuring the change of their length with increasing temperature. For assessing the thermal shock resistance of ceramics test specimens can be heated up to specific temperatures and quenched abruptly and their mechanical strength can be tested in comparison to untreated samples (Tite et al. 2002; Müller et al. 2014).

4.2 Structural Multi-Scale Modelling and Simulation of Performance

While the intrinsic properties of different ceramic materials can be investigated systematically as well as replicably with standard material testing, the extensive properties of objects or structures fabricated from these materials, such as pottery vessels, are considerably more difficult and complex to examine (Kilikoglou & Vekinis 2002). Testing of archaeological ceramic vessels is out of question due to their implicated destruction. On the other hand, the testing of replicates involves essential uncertainties, such as the closeness to the initial design or the selected points of load to be tested according to the intended use. The digital simulation of thermomechanical performance of modelled ceramic vessels under external loads, on the other hand, provides an alternative approach. The performance of a solid structure can be described mathematically as a system of boundary value problems, which in the case of basic shapes can be analytically formulated and evaluated. Because an exact analytical solution, though, is not possible for two- or three-dimensional structures with more complex shape, the problem can be solved with an approximate numerical approach, which is based on the discretization of the structural system (Hughes 2000). The digital model of the structure is divided into a finite number of discrete parts, so-called elements with material properties according to a pre-defined material model. These are connected among each other via a mesh of nodes, which are defined by a series of parameters according to their degrees of freedom (DOF), such as spatial coordinates, stress tensor, temperature, or directional heat flux. Based on material properties, DOFs, and relationships, a system of equations is generated, which under consideration of boundary conditions can be solved by applying the finite element method (FEM) (Zienkiewicz et al. 2005). For an integrated study of vessel performance, FEM can be applied on digital structural models at different scale levels following a bottom-to-top multi-scale approach (LLorca et al. 2011; Hein & Kilikoglou 2025) (Figure 5). The simulation results can be compared and combined with the results from material testing assessing, for example, heat transfer or damage risk of ceramic components under thermomechanical load (Hein & Kilikoglou 2020b).

4.3 Summarizing Material Properties

In order to understand the potential function and use of pottery, their material properties and performance have to be investigated. These depend to a large

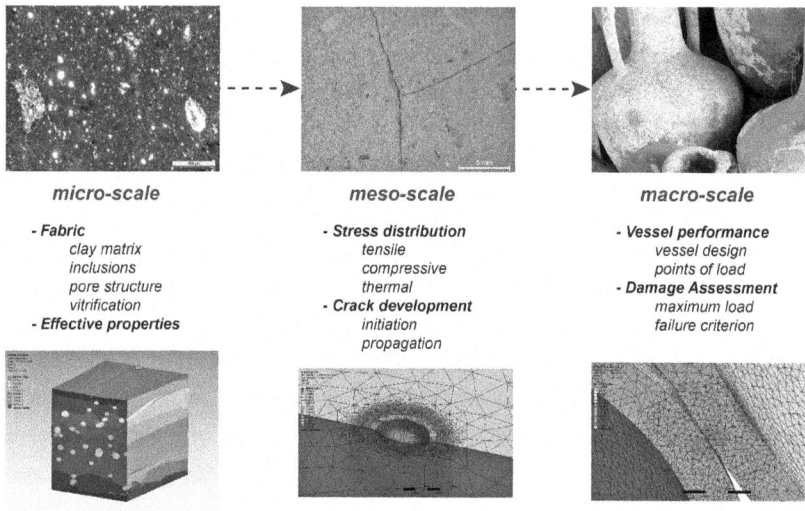

Figure 5 Multiscale modelling of ceramics: Digital models of ceramics at different scale levels and the simulation of their performance under load provide different types of information (Hein & Kilikoglou 2025).

extent on technical choices during the manufacturing process. While the examination of the mineralogical and elemental composition as well as of the petrographic fabric provides information about the initially selected raw materials and added temper materials, the examination of the microstructure provides information about vessel forming and firing conditions. The thermomechanical properties of pottery can be assessed with standard material tests either of specimens cut from authentic ceramic fragments or of replicates of the studied ceramic fabrics. In this way, specific manufacturing parameters can be identified which affect the material performance of the final product. The analytical studies can be complemented with digital modelling on various scale levels. Examination of material performance of structural models under simulated loads allows for a systematic investigation of specific parameters as well as for assessing design and shape parameters, which cannot be directly examined in material tests.

5 Thermoluminescence as a Tool for Age Assessment and Palaeothermometry Studies of Baked Clayey Artefacts

Georgios S. Polymeris

Pottery and ceramic artefacts are the most important materials that could be recovered during the excavation of any archaeological site for its periodization. Stratigraphy allows a relative chronological sequence to be established, based on the physical relationships among excavation layers (Galli et al. 2020).

Besides stratigraphy, in many cases pottery yields a plethora of information that could be used as age indicators for indirect dating, such as type and typology, colouring and painting patterns, and, in some cases, even either the name or the signature of the artist himself; always in conjunction to comparison with written historical texts. Nevertheless, there are many cases where such ceramic findings do not hold any feature useful for chronological use. Towards resolving such problems, archaeological research has been supported by scientific dating techniques. This support was both substantial and prominent during the second half of the 20th century, following the Second World War, when technological advances were really important in physics research.

Scientific age assessment of archaeological remains is essential in archaeological research, in order to place in chronological order findings and civilizations while setting the corresponding chronological context in terms of absolute chronology. It serves as a fundamental point representing the typical intervention of scientific methods in supporting archaeological approach or the study of Cultural Heritage objects. The absolute age of a historical ceramic object is one of the most significant and useful pieces of information, since this can be used to assist the characterization of the site, as well as a crosscheck of the age of a building, structure, or settlement.

5.1 (Thermally) Stimulated Luminescence Dating

5.1.1 General Considerations

Luminescence dating methods encompass a range of techniques, which are capable of determining the age of crystalline and inorganic, semiconducting, non-metal materials such as pottery and kilns. These techniques are based on the radiation-induced charge population within the crystalline minerals, and record the time since the last event when the charge population was reset (Aitken 1985); this is a physical quantity that increases monotonically with time. Samples for luminescence dating can be divided into two groups. The first group includes geological sediments whose grains have been exposed to sunlight during transport or deposition, along with lithic archaeological artefacts that could be dated using surface exposure dating, such as masonry, megalithic buildings and constructions, monolithic structures and monuments, rock art and mortars (Liritzis 2011). The second group includes archaeological samples that consist of clayey materials being heated, burnt, fired, or baked in the past. This group includes ceramics, pottery, porcelain, bricks, kilns, and, in general, fired or even burnt materials, along with solidified lava, volcanic, and siliceous rocks (cherts). In that group, which also includes heated lithics, fire-cracked and fire-modified rocks, heating is the zeroing mechanism, and thus, luminescence can date the last heating event; either accidental or intentional.

All crystalline and inorganic, semiconducting, non-metal minerals are exposed to environmental ionizing radiation ever since they were formed. Radiation causes ionization of atoms in these materials, thus creating free electrons and positive ions simultaneously. The same minerals include a number of either impurities or defects, the distribution of which is such that these act as metastable traps for free electrons inside the main matrix of the mineral. Thus, electrons diffuse through the mineral until they finally get trapped in specific defects of the crystal lattice termed traps. The term 'metastable' is used in order to assign a trapping lifetime to each one of these traps; unless the mineral is externally stimulated, the electrons could stay trapped as long as tenfold the corresponding trap's lifetime. In the case of stimulation, the released electrons once again diffuse through the material until they find positive ions (holes) in the lattice and recombine. Each recombination results in the emission of one photon in the optical wavelength band (400–700 nm). This faint light emitted is called stimulated luminescence. Stimulation can take place either inside the lab or during the overall life cycle of the artefact to be dated. The two main stimulation modes include either heating or the action of light (bleaching). Inside the laboratory, in the former case we have thermoluminescence (TL hereafter) while in the latter optically stimulated luminescence (OSL). While OSL is frequently used for dating materials that are involved within the first group (namely geological dating of sediments and rocks), TL is the most appropriate dating technique for the constituents of the second group.

Focusing now on TL, we shall continue by noticing that it stands as the most effective and well-established technique towards both age assessment of heated/burnt materials as well as authenticity testing of pottery, terracotta, and porcelain (Aitken 1985; Wagner 1998). It is important to emphasize that in general, heating to an adequately high temperature is required in order to have an effective zeroing mechanism and thus reliable ages. This temperature should not be lower than 400–450°C. Nowadays, for dating all these heated materials, TL signal from silt particles is highly recommended; alternatively, the OSL signal of sand-sized quartz is also being used. This section will focus on the application of solely TL for dating ceramics, pottery and in general every clayey material being heated, burnt, fired, or baked in the past.

5.1.2 Thermoluminescence Phenomenon and Main Rationale for Dating

Baked artefacts such as pottery, kilns, ceramics, and sherds include a mixture of fine-grained clays and coarser-grained siliciclastic materials, such as quartz and feldspars (Duller 2008). Pottery is made by firing clays, which contain 40–60% silica. Most of it is in the crystalline form of quartz; nevertheless, depending on the origin of the clay, feldspar is also an important constituent mineral. These two naturally occurring minerals contain a plethora of traps, among which, and without any external stimulation, some yield lifetimes so short that these are not useful for dating applications. Nevertheless, some could be stable enough to store electrons for extremely long time intervals, depending upon specific physical characteristics of the material. Consequently, thermoluminescence dating is based on the fact that naturally occurring minerals like quartz and feldspars act as natural dosimeters and preserve a record of irradiation energy received through time.

In order to quantify this deposited energy, the concept of accumulated dose (in units of Gy), namely energy per unit mass, is used. Excluding radiation accidents and artificial irradiation because of everyday applications, minerals in general are irradiated by (a) decay of natural radionuclides that exist in their environment of deposition, (b) decay of natural radionuclides within the materials themselves, and finally (c) gamma radiation from cosmic rays. For both decays inside and in the surrounding of the materials, this dose results mainly from the decay of natural radionuclides such as ^{232}Th, ^{40}K, ^{87}Rb, and natural U (both ^{235}U and ^{238}U), along with cosmic rays. All these provide a source of low-level ionizing radiation through time that could be considered stable when compared to the overall irradiation time.

The number of trapped electrons is increasing as long as the material is irradiated, without being stimulated. The total amount of trapped charge is proportional to the total radiation energy absorbed by the materials, and therefore to the time subjected to irradiation. The intensity of the luminescence light is also proportional to the total radiation energy absorbed by the materials, and therefore to the time subjected to irradiation (Aitken 1985, 1990). However, for the case of any archaeological artefact, every time that this is subjected to prolonged heating, as in the case of firing, electrons are abruptly evicted and traps are totally emptied; thus, TL signal is totally zeroed. In that case, the material is said to be totally reset. Afterwards, it could start accumulating energy in the form of trapped electrons in order to refill the empty traps once again. The total number of trapped electrons forms a luminescent 'clock' which starts measuring time from the beginning (t = 0) every time that these traps are totally emptied. Thus, the last heating signifies the zeroing event of the 'time-clock', while the duration of irradiation since the last zeroing effect is associated with the age since then.

Towards the direction of TL age determination, two different physical quantities are required: the total accumulated dose over the past, signifying the total amount of energy deposited inside the matrix, termed paleodose, as well as the rate at which this energy-dose is accumulated, termed dose rate

(DR). To be more precise, the concept of equivalent dose is used (D_e, in Gy units), standing as the amount of irradiation dose from either β or γ radiation, which is needed in order to obtain a luminescence signal identical to that resulting from natural radiation exposure. This is a physical quantity that increases monotonically with time and can be measured precisely. The ratio of these two quantities, that is, the equivalent dose over the dose-rate, represents the age of the sample.

$$Age\ (kyrs) = \frac{Equivalent\ Dose}{Dose\ Rate} = \frac{D_e\ (Gy)}{DR\left(\frac{Gy}{kyrs}\right)}$$

5.1.3 Sampling Guidelines

As the materials in question are quite compact, it is not mandatory to keep them in the dark before sampling. Nevertheless, samples should be sealed in an airtight plastic bag as soon as they are excavated. Most laboratories require sampling of thick samples, with sizes $\geq$ 10 mm thick and 30–40 mm across (Nelson et al. 2015). Generally, larger-sized samples result in ages with better precision. When it is possible, multiple sherds/parts of the same object should be collected so that statistics will result in decreased error and uncertainty; this becomes feasible when kilns are to be dated (Aidona et al. 2021). Finally, in many cases drilling could also be considered as an alternative sampling strategy. In these cases, it is suggested that the drill should be at least 50 mm in diameter while sampling should take place to depths of 100 mm. This will provide an adequate length after discarding the outer 1–2 mm of the core affected by the drilling. This strategy follows on directly from Fleming (1979), who had suggested drilling as sampling strategy for authenticity testing in pottery; drilling was, and is still supposed to take place from a surface underneath the artefact, at 10 mm in diameter and to depths of 10 mm.

Very fine silt clay yields grains with diameter less than 20 μm while coarse-grained sand includes grains with dimension over 90 μm. The use of small samples (including some hundreds of grains) and single-grain dating of purified coarse grains of either quartz or feldspar have several advantages over polymineral fine-grained dating (4–12 μm); the former is routinely used in OSL dating of sediments, while the latter is the standard procedure for TL dating of previously heated materials. After collecting those, the samples are treated inside the laboratory strictly under red dim light conditions. The outer 2- to 4-mm-thick outer layer of the sample should be mechanically removed, in order to eliminate the light-subjected portions (Fleming 1979; Aitken 1985; 1990). The exact thickness to be removed depends strongly on the colour of the sample and thus its opacity; the darker the colour, the less sample should be removed. Application of standard chemical procedures is suggested when silt material is preferred (for an example the readers could refer to Vieillevigne et al. 2007). The final step includes gently crushing the sample in an agate pestle and mortar. Finally, both extraction of grains within the grain size range 4–12 μm and final homogeneous precipitation onto 1-cm-diameter aluminium discs is performed by suspension in acetone as the solvent evaporates according to the settling procedure described by Zimmerman (1971). The sample on each disc is termed an aliquot.

The sample's dose rate could be assessed by calculating the magnitude of the accumulated radiation dose that contributes to the material itself, from factors such as cosmic rays and radioactive elements from the surrounding soil. Thus, sampling should also include the soil closely surrounding the artefact, enabling the measurement of both gamma dose rate and water content. Even though this soil sample also need not be kept in the dark, it should be sealed in an airtight plastic bag as soon as from the first moments of the excavation so that the water content is preserved. Information on the latitude, longitude, and elevation of the site along with the burial depth of the sample is also mandatory so that the cosmic ray contribution to the dose rate could be calculated. In cases where samples must be collected near a context boundary, such as an infill and the natural soil, in situ measurements of the gamma dose rate are strongly suggested (Duller 2008). This could be achieved by using either a portable gamma spectrometer or capsule TL dosimeters.

5.1.4 Measuring Thermoluminescence: The Concept of the TL Glow Curve and the Connection to the Traps

While measuring TL, heating is conducted from room temperature up to usually 500°C, with a stable, low heating rate ($\leq 5°C/s$). The intensity of the signal is recorded versus temperature and is so weak that it could be measurable only by means of a sufficiently sensitive device called photomultiplier. The temperature dependence of the emission appears as a set of peaks with each one corresponding to an electron-trapping defect; this is the definition of the TL glow curve. TL glow curves in some cases consist of well-defined peaks and in others, of complex sets of overlapping peaks. Each TL peak corresponds to an electron trap of the material under study. TL peaks at low temperatures correspond to shallow electron traps that are unstable with low lifetimes as they can be excited easily. TL peaks at high temperatures correspond to deeper traps which are considered as stable, as they yield lifetimes exceeding some thousands or even hundreds of thousands of years. For a second heating of the same sample without further irradiation, the emission curve consists only of black body radiation and is characterized as a background measurement.

5.1.5 Measurements for TL Dating inside the Laboratory

Equivalent Dose

For the calculation of the equivalent dose (D_e) of pottery samples, the multiple-aliquot, additive dose (MAAD) procedure in TL is usually applied (Aitken 1985; Wagner 1998). In the framework of this technique, the silt size fraction of each pottery sample is divided into (at least) 16 to 20 separate aliquots. These aliquots are divided into 4 groups and independently irradiated to regenerate an individual TL glow curve each. Each group, consisting of 4 to 5 aliquots, corresponds to a unique additive dose. The term 'additive' is used as each dose is attributed over the naturally accrued TL signal. At least three different artificial (additive) doses are attributed, plus a zero Gy additive dose, corresponding to the natural TL (NTL hereafter) signal; this is the signal that is attributed to the irradiation solely during the past. For this group of NTL measurements, more aliquots could be used, as reproducibility is crucial. Doses usually range from zero Gy (for the group of the NTL) up to 20 Gy, in steps of either 5 or 7 Gy. A background signal measurement, also known as reheat, should be measured for each aliquot and thus subtracted from the corresponding TL glow curve. Mass reproducibility for all discs-aliquots should be kept within ±3–5%; the same is expected for the TL glow curves of each group. Finally, following measurements of the NTL signal, a low dose is applied to each aliquot of the respective group, to check for supralinearity corrections (I). These low doses range between 0.5 and 7.5 Gy; each dose is attributed to different disc-aliquot.

Dose Rate

The dose rate is calculated based on the decay of all aforementioned naturally occurring radionuclides inside both the artefacts' clay matrix and the corresponding surrounding soil. The most widely used method to estimate the dose rate (in units of Gy/kyrs) includes measuring the sample's content of radioactive elements (^{232}Th, ^{40}K, ^{87}Rb, and natural U) and calculating the amount of radiation that these release per time unit by using the appropriate conversion factors (Aitken 1985, Appendix F; Liritzis et al. 2013). Assuming radioactive equilibrium, this equals the rate of radiation that is absorbed as well. The calculation considers the possible presence of water as it attenuates ionizing radiation, and the amount of cosmic radiation that reaches the sample at a given depth below ground surface (Liritzis et al. 2015). Dose rate expresses the annual radiation dose (Liritzis et al. 2013). The most sophisticated methods to calculate the dose rate, such as gamma spectroscopy and inductively charged plasma mass spectroscopy (ICP-MS), enable measuring the sample's content of all radioactive member isotopes of the radioactive chains individually. Nevertheless, as an alternative, measurements of the content of the main radioactive isotopes could result in dose rate calculations. Natural Uranium and ^{232}Th are usually measured efficiently with the aid of thick source alpha counting, while ^{40}K and ^{87}Rb using micro-X-ray fluorescence (μXRF), flame atomic absorption spectroscopy (FAAS), and scanning electron microscopy coupled with energy dispersive X-ray spectroscopy (SEM-EDX).

5.1.6 Data Analysis inside the Laboratory

For each pottery sample, discs are irradiated in groups of four or five at each dose; thus, reproducibility of at least three different TL glow curves for each group is highly recommended. Figure 6 presents typical as well as representative MAAD TL analysis results for a kiln sample reported by Aidona et al. (2018). The plot in Figure 6A presents typical additive dose TL curves, each one being the mean value of at least three independently measured glow curves; additive doses are presented in the plot. Error bars indicate excellent reproducibility among the glow curves of the same group-dose. It is highly recommended that the TL signal presents a linear response over increasing doses. Such linearity should be strongly established; this could be achieved by calculating the dose–response slope (S) throughout the entire TL glow curve and subsequently plot it versus temperature for each one of the different additive doses attributed. This slope is calculated according to the following formula (Liritzis et al. 2015; Aidona et al. 2018):

$$S = \frac{[(NTL+\beta_i)-(NTL)]}{\beta_i} \left(\frac{TL\ Counts}{Gy}\right)$$

where ($NTL + \beta_i$) denotes the corresponding TL glow curves after each additive dose (β_i) has been administered. The preceding subtraction takes place for each data point. A single individual S curve corresponding to each additive dose is yielded. In the case of linearity, these individual S curves should coincide over an extended temperature region of the glow curve, as the case presented in Figure 6B. This stands among the most important criterion for selecting the appropriate signal integration region of interest for age calculation. The inset of this plot presents a representative example of additive (squares) and second glow (diamonds) TL build up curves for the temperature of 250°C. Equivalent doses are estimated, in units of Gy, according to the following equation:

$$D_e = \frac{NTL}{S}\left(\frac{TL\ Counts}{\frac{TL\ Counts}{Gy}}\right)$$

Once again, the preceding calculation takes place for each data point, over the entire TL glow curve temperature region. For prolonged heating, the plots of equivalent dose versus temperature are expected to yield wide plateaus, with the

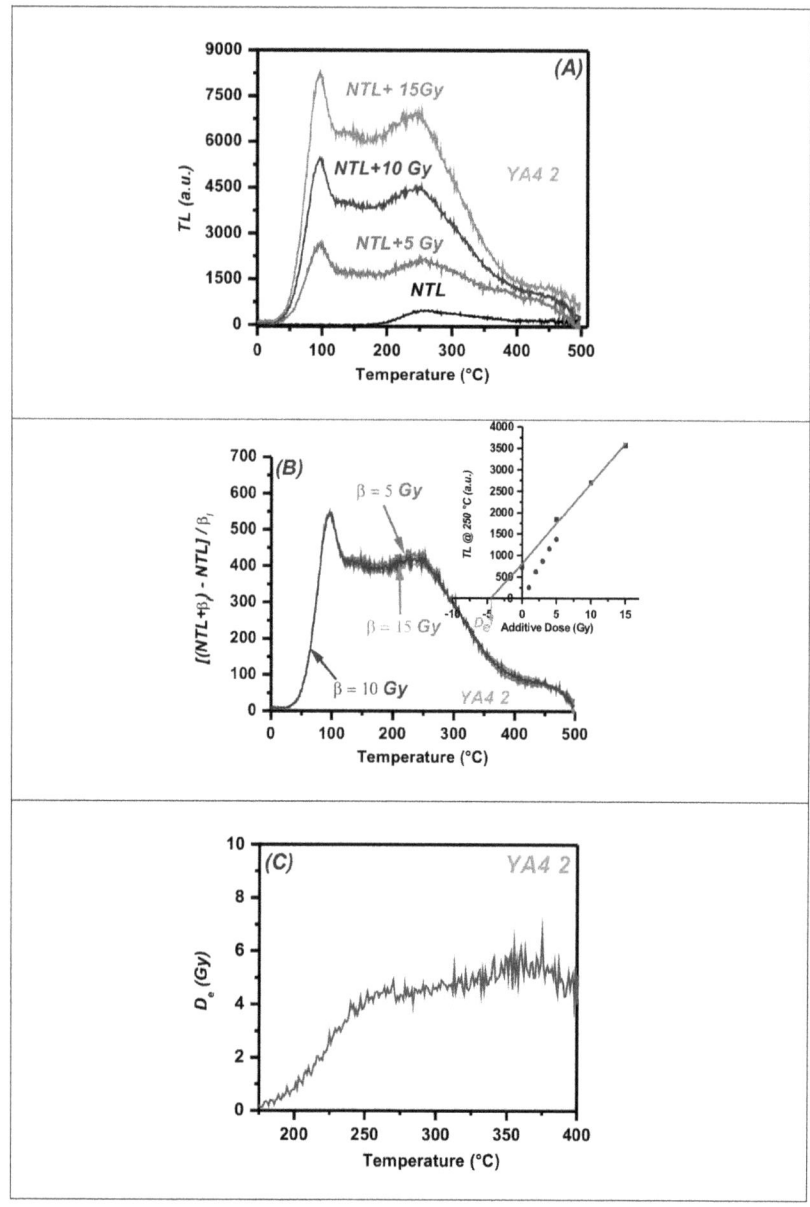

Figure 6 Plot (A) presents examples of TL glow curves of the additive dose procedure, namely natural TL along with three additive glow curves (5, 10, and 15 Gy, respectively). Reheats have been subtracted. Each TL glow curve is expressed in terms of the average over at least three individual TL glow curves. Plot (B) presents the dose-response-slope curve S of TL versus temperature, for the three additive doses applied. Inset shows additive dose growth curves for the

equivalent dose final values being obtained as the mean value over the plateaus for each sample. A typical plot of D_e against glow curve temperature is presented in Figure 6C. Supra-linearity correction, I, is equal to zero if the second glow TL dose–response passes from the origin of both axes; otherwise, this non-zero value is added to the equivalent dose.

5.1.7 Errors, Error Sources, and Limitations

Estimation of accuracy is a particularly tedious aspect in TL dating of pottery. The first important error source is possible poor reproducibility in mass among the aliquots. As a large number of aliquots are being used for getting one single age, reproducibility becomes quite important. Moreover, a dozen or so measured quantities enter into the corresponding calculation, each one among them incorporating the corresponding uncertainty. Thus, the overall uncertainty should reflect the combined effect of uncertainties in these, appropriately weighted (Aitken 1990). Errors are also derived from the uncertainties in curve fitting, especially when lack of linearity is monitored. Whereas the overall random errors on a date can be reduced by averaging the results on a number of synchronous samples, this is quite difficult for the systematic uncertainties. Based on all aforementioned, the latter is the ultimate barrier to better accuracy, presently being of the order $\pm\ 7$–10% at the 68% confidence level ($\pm 1\sigma$).

TL dating can reach back to the earliest pottery and even beyond; how much beyond depends on both properties and origin of the mineral being used. TL ages of baked clay around 30 to 50 kyrs could be easily achieved, while the technique has reported ages as old as 300 kyrs before the current era. At the recent end of the age range limitation, pottery and baked clay objects that are few hundred years old can be safely dated using the previously described procedure, always depending on the levels of both radioactivity and TL sensitivity.

5.1.8 Ages and Interpretation

For the majority of pottery and ceramic items, last heating coincides with the heating while manufacturing the artefact. For ceramics belonging to an archaeological site, dating obtained by scientific techniques is used as a terminus

---

Caption for Figure 6 (cont.)

temperature of 320°C, for both first (squares) and second glow (points) measurements. The arrow indicates the D_e value. Supra-linearity correction I is estimated to be zero. Plot (C) presents D_e versus temperature, indicating a long plateau (Reproduced from Aidona et al. 2018; their figure 7).

post-quem and combined with the stratigraphic sequence, in order to frame the life of the excavated site into an absolute chronological range. Nevertheless, studies on ceramics are usually wide enough, dealing with the investigation of their overall life cycle, from the acquisition and processing of raw materials to production and distribution, through their use, possible reuse, and discard, along with interpretation in terms of the people producing, distributing, and using them (Galli et al. 2020). This case of discard becomes quite important for kilns, where last heating is closely related to the last time of labour. A very interesting case includes furnaces that had been used for smelting metals (Nerantzis et al. 2017); furnace fragments and refractories of severely fired clay, which are usually present in such production sites, represent an ideal material for dating the metallurgical activity.

Nevertheless, TL is the unique dating technique that can identify possible reuse of ceramic items. A very interesting feature is yielded while estimating the equivalent dose values, indicating two individual plateaus in the corresponding plots versus temperature. The secondary plateau is observed at higher temperatures than that of the primary and main plateau, corresponding at the same time to a larger equivalent dose and thus to an older age. The presence of two plateaus resulting for the same sample identifies two independent zeroing events in the past, in conjunction to insufficient heating of the sample recently, namely heating at firing temperatures around or lower than 500°C. The second, milder zeroing event due to insufficient heating is usually interpreted as either a fire event in recent history or a reuse period of the artefact (Liritzis et al. 2015).

When possible, the application of more dating techniques, together with the available archaeological evidence, offers the best approach for obtaining a more precise chronological framework for an archaeological site. Archaeomagnetic and TL dating techniques share the same rationale, dating exactly the same event that is the last heating of the artefacts baked at high temperature. During the last years, the archaeomagnetic method is considered as complementary dating tool for baked clay to TL, not only in cases where other more traditional dating methods failed to estimate the age of the structures but also due to its capacity to date directly the structures themselves and not findings they contain (Kontopoulou et al. 2015; Aidona et al. 2018, 2021).

5.2 Thermoluminescence for Palaeothermometry

5.2.1 Mineralogy of Quartz

As pottery contains 40–60% silica, most of it being in the crystalline form, the presence of quartz is ubiquitous, in all ceramic samples. Given that it is one of the most abundant minerals occurring at the Earth's crust, it is not surprising that it generally represents the prevalent phase in ceramics. At ambient temperatures, α-quartz crystallizes to a trigonal polymorph and is stable up to 573°C; this is the temperature threshold for the transition of α-quartz to β-quartz. This latter phase crystallizes in a hexagonal form and is also stable. In fact, this transition is reversible involving a volume decrease and, during cooling, β-quartz transforms back into α-quartz (Preusser et al. 2010). If the temperature reaches 872°C, β-quartz transforms into HP-tridymite which later on transforms into β-cristobalite at 1470°C (Heaney 1994). Transition from β-quartz to tridymite is irreversible and thus tridymite cannot transform back to β-quartz. However, the tridymite transformation is bypassed when firing pure quartz; in this case, in fact, β-cristobalite is directly formed at ~ 1050°C, and this transition is reversible (Heaney 1994; Gliozzo 2020). Quartz appears to be stable up to high temperatures of about 850–900°C, and as it proceeds towards higher temperatures, its amounts can gradually or abruptly decrease. The mineralogy of quartz can provide useful firing temperature thresholds, based on the detected quartz polymorphs, the corresponding transition temperatures, and the formation of new phases depending on the surrounding established minerals. Nevertheless, the following sections will describe an alternative and innovative experimental approach for the assessment of firing temperature of pottery, presenting a methodology that takes full advantage of TL properties of quartz (Sunta & David 1982). For other techniques towards assessment of firing temperature in the past, either mainstream or alternative, the readers could refer to Gliozzo (2020).

5.2.2 Rationale

Quartz mineral, besides being a good dosimeter-chronometer, ubiquitous, and resistant to weathering, is the most widely used mineral for TL that exhibits some quite interesting properties: (a) under the combined action of irradiation and heating, the sensitivity of the TL signal (namely the quantity of TL per unit mass and dose) does not remain constant but increases instead; this is the so-called pre-dose sensitization (Zimmerman 1971; Bailiff 1994). This effect involves simultaneous sensitization due to both thermal and dose contribution to the 110°C TL peak pre-dose method (Bailiff 1994); (b) it can retain information regarding its thermal history in terms of the maximum temperature attained (Sanjurjo-Sanchez et al. 2018). These unique as well as prevalent properties of all quartz samples all around Earth have been exploited in the past to assess the firing temperature of pottery. While measuring TL in quartz, the corresponding glow curve shows mainly four main peaks with maximum intensities at 110°C, 200°C, 325°C, and 375°C (at moderate heating rates; Franklin et al. 1995).

The 110°C TL peak, being correlated to a shallow trap, is useless for dating. Nevertheless, the luminescence characteristics of the 110°C peak can be directly correlated to the thermal history of quartz and specifically to the firing temperature (Watson & Aitken 1985).

The sensitization of the 110°C TL peak of quartz occurs within the temperature range over 200°C, provided that this temperature does not exceed 880°C where the phase transition of β-quartz (to tridymite) is irreversible. Higher temperatures can cause vitrification and high-temperature minerals that easily allow identifying the firing temperature, mostly using SEM. Once a pottery sample is re-annealed (or re-fired) in the laboratory at a temperature that is higher than the firing temperature of the original pottery sample (where from quartz was extracted) sensitization of the 110°C peak's TL intensity is observed. The underlying idea of the 110°C TL peak sensitization method is that thermally induced hole transfer of charge associated with geological irradiation takes place during firing, and re-firing experiments can reconstruct the point at which additional sensitization takes place. Even though the signal of the high-temperature TL peaks could also be effectively used for thermometry (Spencer & Sanderson 2012; Oniya et al. 2012; Polymeris et al. 2014), especially for temperatures over 600°C, the 110°C TL peak is suggested as the best probe. From a practical point of view, the use of this specific signal is quite useful, as this is a single, ubiquitous, and prominent peak that does not require deconvolution analysis.

However, there are a number of requirements for such behaviour to work – including the need for thermal stable hole reservoirs (from which the initial firing can transfer charge carriers) in sufficient supply that they do not saturate under geological conditions, and that the luminescence centres should be thermally stable over archaeological timescales so that such information is preserved. These requirements are not always fulfilled while the conditions required for effective application cannot be assured in advance.

5.2.3 Sampling, Handling, and TL Measurements

For palaeothermometry applications, the most external layer of the pottery samples should be removed in order to remove possible corrosion and oxidation products. About 5 gr of each sample should be scraped off and gently crushed. For TL analyses, use of 90–250 μm grain-size is suggested to get enough quartz amounts, whereas the 90–180 μm grain-size fraction is recommended (Polymeris et al. 2014).

Towards obtaining pure coarse quartz extracts, the samples are sieved to get the 90–250 μm grain-size fraction; grains are water-washed and treated with

HCl and H_2O_2 to remove carbonates and any remaining organic matter, respectively. Heavy liquids of densities 2.62 and 2.70 g/cm^3 should be used to separate feldspars, quartz, and heavy minerals. HF application to the quartz extract removes any feldspar grains, and HCl is applied again after water-washing to remove any remaining soluble fluorides.

Initially, each pottery sample should be divided into a number of segments. Each segment is to be annealed (or re-fired) at a different temperature, in steps of 50°C. The selection of the appropriate temperature region depends strongly on the samples to be studied, with the prerequisite that should bracket the original firing temperature. Preliminary mineralogical analysis could constrain this aforementioned temperature range. Annealing can be performed in external automatic furnaces. The annealing duration in all cases should be at least 1 hour in an oxygen atmosphere; this is the typical firing duration for pottery. Independent of the temperature, in all cycles, the heating that is applied inside the laboratory is termed re-firing.

Historically, the first protocol that was experimentally applied was the protocol of Thermal Activation Curves (TAC) by Göksu et al. (1989) in TL. Subsequent work has demonstrated that the full pre-dose protocol suggested by Polymeris et al. (2014 and references therein) is much more robust and was successfully used to assess the firing temperature of pottery samples. This protocol has also been proven reliable for fired stones (Sanjurjo-Sánchez et al. 2013). This protocol includes three sequential cycles of dose and TL measurements, designed to monitor the dependence of both sensitivity and sensitization of the 110°C TL peak due to (a) the thermal contribution of the pre-dose effect (Koul et al. 2010) and (b) the full pre-dose effect to gradually increasing heating. Each TL measurement should be performed at low heating rate, up to a maximum temperature of 500°C. Figure 7 presents an example of TL glow curves measured in the framework of this optimized protocol up to 500°C, following a selection of re-firing temperatures. This figure presents fully pre-dosed TL glow curves that were measured during the third cycle of dose and measurement. For more details, the readers could refer to protocol (A) from Polymeris et al. (2014).

The working principle includes studying the temperature-dependent changes of both thermal and pre-dose sensitization of the 110°C TL peak in quartz due to re-firing. The plot of the "110 °C TL peak" sensitization versus re-firing temperature, normalized over the respective sensitivity at the lowest re-firing temperature is a very useful tool. No sensitization takes place at low re-firing temperatures, as the normalized sensitivity of the probe peak gets values around 1. As long as this latter temperature is lower than (or even equal to) the firing temperature in the past, the intensity of the 110°C TL peak doesn't change. By the time that re-firing

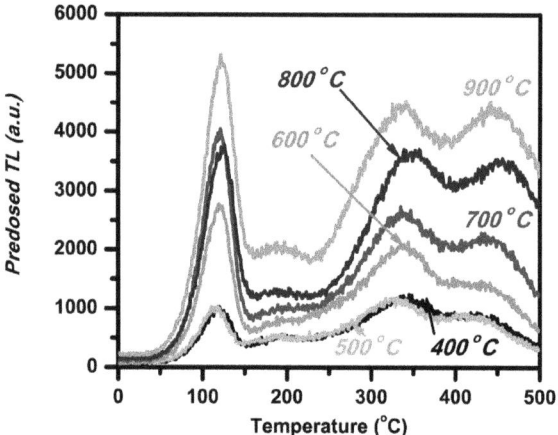

Figure 7 Example of pre-dosed TL glow curves for quartz extracted from Mesopotamian pottery samples; each curve is the average of three independent measurements. Arithmetic indicates the re-firing temperature (Reproduced from Polymeris et al. 2014; their figure 1).

temperature in the lab becomes higher than the firing temperature, re-firing temperature dominates due to being higher than the temperature of the maximum heating, inducing sensitization; thus, a prominent and steep increase in both sensitivity and sensitization is monitored. At these temperatures, a prominent spike is observed when this ratio is plotted versus re-firing temperature. However, for this latter plot, typical experimental features, such as the monotonic increase of the sensitization ratio above the annealing temperature along with a decrease at re-firing temperature around 900°C, are expected (Koul 2006; Polymeris et al. 2007, 2014).

All these features are obvious in Figure 8 that presents the results of the TL analysis in terms of the normalized 110°C TL versus the initial re-firing temperature obtained for one ancient ceramic coffin of a Japanese Emperor (Tema et al. 2024). The TL sensitivity of the 110°C TL peak does not depend on the laboratory re-firing temperature up to 525°C, representing the last re-firing temperature that indicates the last stable (normalized) sensitivity. As re-firing temperature in the lab increases further, all three sensitivities show a steep increase, with the one due to pre-dose sensitization being the most prominent. This increase of sensitivity is not linear versus the re-firing temperature, which is a typical feature of firing temperature below 550°C. In such cases, the maximum heating temperature is considered as the temperature just before this prominent and steep sensitivity change, estimating

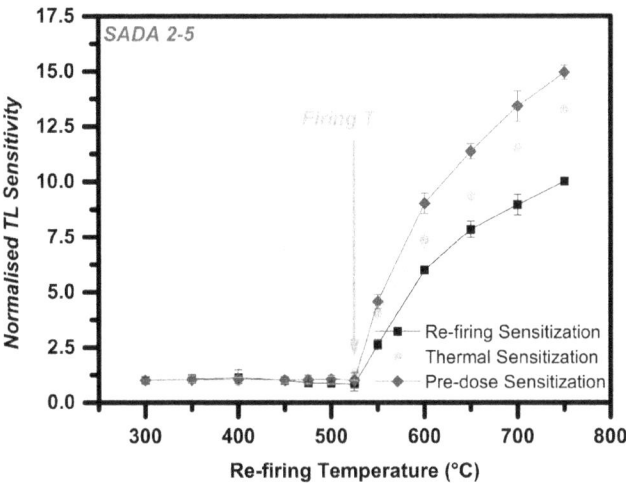

Figure 8 Normalized TL sensitivity versus laboratory re-firing temperatures for the 110°C TL peak measured from one sample of an ancient ceramic coffin of a Japanese emperor. Normalization has been carried out over the corresponding first data point. The plots represent re-firing sensitization (squares), thermal sensitization (dots), and pre-dose sensitization (diamonds). Re-firing, thermal, and pre-dose sensitizations are recorded at various re-firing temperatures in the range between 300°C and 750°C in steps of 50°C (Reproduced from E. Tema et al. 2024; their figure 4).

in this case firing temperature of around 525±25°C; an error of ±25°C is considered as the smallest re-firing temperature step used in the luminescence protocol.

5.3 Considerations and Limitations

The method indicates the maximum temperature that a ceramic has sensed, even if this latter was true for a short period compared to the overall firing duration. Consistency and compatibility of the TL results with the results obtained from other techniques, such as XRD, FTIR, and SEM data, will provide hints towards the duration. This is quite important in cases where pottery is produced on a massive scale, probably in specific production centres; the firing conditions (including temperature, redox, and time) should be very similar or even standardized. Heterogeneous temperature distribution inside the kilns becomes a major issue. A batch of pots is expected to differ in the temperature reached depending on different conditions such as size of the kiln, fuel, air flux, and the number of pots in the same kiln volume. Especially for the former parameter, the range of temperature variation within the same kiln during a single firing can be as high as 200°C (Maggetti et al. 2011; Kontopoulou et al. 2015). Therefore, the range of temperature variation among pots in the same batch is variable depending on the pot location in a kiln.

Possible low luminescence sensitivity of the signals could, in general, be a drawback for the technique, resulting in features such as lack of a systematic increasing trend in the luminescence sensitivity versus annealing temperature (Sanjurjo-Sánchez et al. 2018). Nevertheless, this latter feature stands as another, indirect indicator towards a moderate firing temperature range; in this case, quartz is definitely of alpha type that has not undergone the transition to beta quartz (Preusser et al. 2009). Appropriate selection of the pre-dose (dose in the second cycle) is mandatory in order to avoid saturation and thus violation of the major requirement for the operational luminescence technique. It is important that the study uses the 110°C peak that is the most sensitive peak to low beta radiation doses.

6 Specific Types of Ceramics: Analysis of Glazed Surfaces

Judit Molera & Trinitat Pradell

The study of glazes provides direct information on their chemical composition and microstructure. This gives a great deal of information on the technical skills of local potters, firing traditions, the trade in specific materials not found locally, the connection or lack of connection between regions, and the introduction and adoption of new trends. In this section, we present an overview of the main constituents of glazes, their microstructures, the main crystalline phases developed during firing, the most common crystals associated with colouring agents (Sn, Mn, Fe, Cu, Co) and how to analyse them.

6.1 Introduction to Glazes

A ceramic glaze is a thin glassy layer fused to the surface of a ceramic[3] body by firing. Transparent glazes are non-crystalline (or amorphous) solids formed from a melt by cooling to the rigidity (*glass transition* temperature) without crystallization. However, bubbles, particles partially dissolved and other reaction compounds developed during the glaze firing, are also often present in the glaze and affect the transparency and colour of the glazes (Figure 9). In addition, the interaction between the glaze and the ceramic body results in the interdiffusion of elements from the glaze into the body and from the body into the glaze. The interaction region (called interface) may be neat or filled with crystals formed by the reaction between paste and glaze, depending on the firing temperature, single or double firing, and composition of paste and glaze.

---

[3] https://en.wikipedia.org/wiki/Ceramic

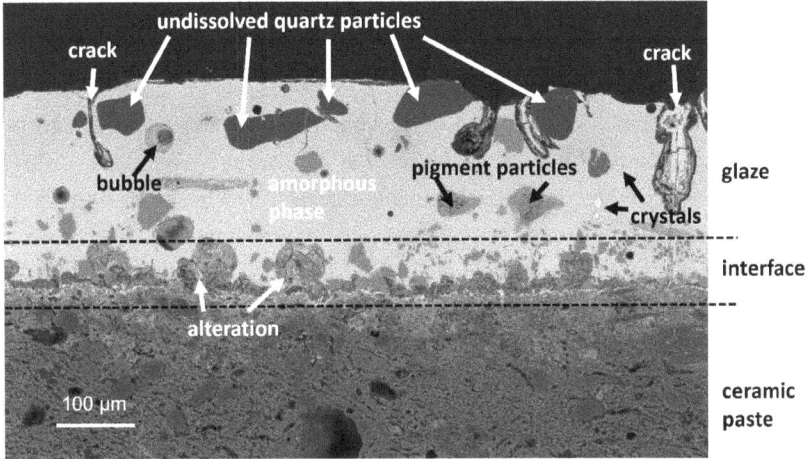

Figure 9 SEM image of a cross section of the glaze showing the microstructure.

As a result, the glazes are not homogeneous and show internal microstructure and chemical composition gradients across the glaze thickness due to diffusion. In addition, the pigments applied to the decorations are prone to dissolve or crystallize depending on the original composition of the pigment and the composition of the glaze, the way they are applied, and the firing conditions (temperature, firing atmosphere, time, etc.). For this reason, the microstructure of the glazes and good analyses of the amorphous phase and crystalline compounds could reveal the firing process and technological choices. The skills of the potters are revealed in the glazing technique, and the firing conditions are also reflected in the glaze microstructure.

6.2 Methodology for Analysing Glazes

There are several methods to analyse glazes. One approach is to analyse it from the surface. By observing the glaze from the surface with a stereoscope or an optical microscope with reflected light, it is possible to determine the pattern of cracks, the presence of bubbles, and crystalline phases. It also provides valuable insights on the state of conservation of the glazes. By using portable X-ray fluorescence (XRF) equipment a chemical analysis of the major elements can be performed. A large area of the glaze is examined, providing an overall composition that includes the amorphous phase, undissolved compounds, and new crystalline phases. Many colourants are present in minor or trace amounts, so *LA-ICP-MS* (laser ablation inductively coupled plasma mass spectrometry) can be used to detect trace elements in glazes. LA-ICP-MS (typical size of the area analysed 20–50 μm and 2–5 μm) is also useful for the determination of boron, which is often present in low levels and may come from natural flux sources or be deliberately added to reduce firing temperatures in enamels. However, it is important to note that the outermost micrometres of the glaze may have a different composition compared to the bulk due to exposure to gases during the heating process. In addition, glazes can be altered by burial conditions, leading to the leaching of certain elements. Typically, elements such as Na, K, and even Pb are prone to leaching, and the alteration compounds often precipitate in the bubbles and cracks or on the glaze surface. Finally, in the case of thin glazes, the penetration of the beam may reach the underlying ceramic surface (typical penetration of X-Rays of 30 keV in a lead-alkali glaze is ~120 μm) as shown in Figure 10A. Therefore, surface analysis should be considered with caution, and the detectors should be specifically calibrated.

In order to carry out a comprehensive analysis of a glaze, it is necessary to make a *cross section* to observe its internal microstructure, which in combination with a micro-analytical technique can be used to analyse the areas of interest. Using *thin sections or polished sections*, a detailed study can be carried out under an optical and electronic microscope, allowing for the detection of bubbles, crystalline phases, and corrosion products (Figure 9 and Figure 10A). SEM examination provides a higher magnification of the structures present (size below the micrometre), and images can be obtained from the detection of the backscattered electrons (BSD) or secondary electrons (SED). BSD provides images with chemical contrast, that is, lighter elements produce less emission and appear darker than heavier elements. However, the penetration of the beam is greater than with the SED detector. SED images provide a higher lateral resolution of surface structures, what is usually called topographic contrast, while maintaining chemical contrast to some extent. The use of a field emission filament, field emission SEM (FE SEM), provides a higher resolution (typically of about 10–20 nm with SED) compared to a normal thermal emission filament (typically of about 10–20 μm with SED) (Figure 10B-C).

Chemical analysis of the amorphous phase, undissolved particles, and newly formed crystallites should be carried out on selected areas of interest, while avoiding areas prone to alteration, bubbles, and cracks, by an energy-dispersive X-ray spectrometer attached to the SEM (SEM-EDS) and microprobe, specifically calibrated. *SEM-EDS*, with a typical detection limit of about 0.1%, is suitable for the analysis of elements present in major and some minor amounts and which is usually less than the inhomogeneity of the glazes. However, detection limits can be affected by overlapping emission lines, especially for metals and heavy elements. *Microprobe*, with a typical detection limit of about 0.01%, offers greater accuracy and reliability for overlapping elements. However, the use of high energies (15 or 20 keV beams) limits the accuracy

Ceramic Analysis 51

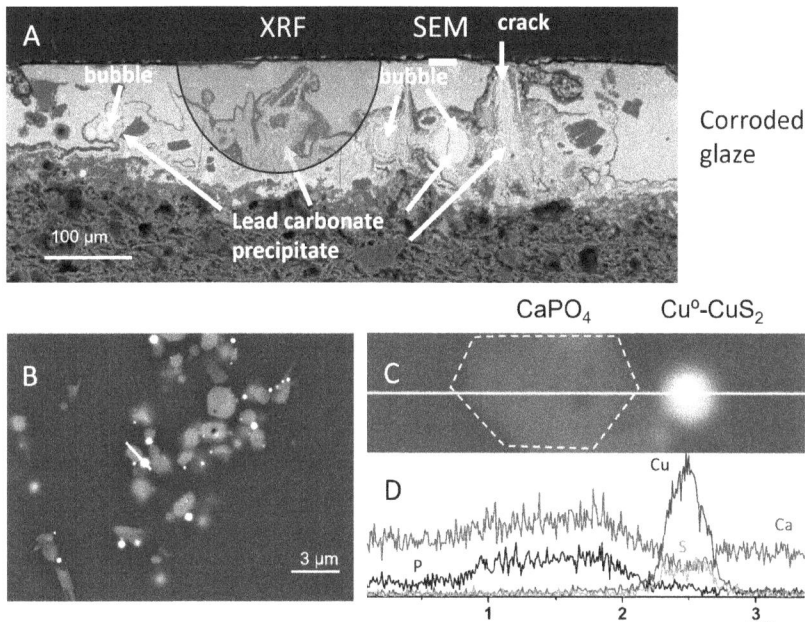

Figure 10 SEM-BSD image of a lead glaze. (A) The penetration of 30 keV X-rays typical of XRF analysis (87% of the beam) for a glaze with a composition of 45% PbO, 35% SiO_2, 5% Al_2O_3, 5% CaO, 5% K_2O, 5% FeO is 120 μm. The penetration of 20 keV electrons typical for SEM-EDS analysis (90% of the beam) is 5.2 μm (B and C). Microcrystals of calcium phosphate and of copper and copper sulphide nanoparticles. (D) EDS line-scan analysis of the yellow line marked in C and D.

for light elements (Z < 10), such as lithium or boron, which are also often present in small amounts in glazes. It's important to note that the analysed spot has a *pear-shaped volume*, with the depth primarily determined by the beam energy and the surface area influenced by the detected element and X-ray energy. The minimal analysed area depends on electron penetration, which also follows a typical pear shape, ranging from 1 to 10 μm based on the glaze composition (e.g., ~5 μm for 20 keV electrons in a lead-alkali glaze; see Figure 10A). This limits the size of the smallest crystallite or particle that can be analysed and the smallest glaze heterogeneity that can be determined. In the case of glazes, the high mobility of certain elements, particularly alkalis such as sodium, can be a significant problem. This can be overcome by measuring a small area rather than a spot, or by slightly defocusing the electron beam. It is also possible to gain lateral accuracy using line-scans or map-scans (1D and 2D), see Figure 10B-D.

Crystalline compounds in glazes can be identified by using *X-ray Diffraction* (XRD) (Figure 11), which can be performed on the glaze surface if it is sufficiently flat. However, the depth of penetration of X-rays into the glaze is relatively small and can reach tens of microns depending on the composition, limiting the identification of compounds near the glaze-ceramic interface. To overcome this limitation, transmission μ-XRD using synchrotron light with a spot size of a few microns in size allows access to different areas of the thin cross section of the glaze with micrometric resolution (Pradell et al. 2013).

Micro-Raman Spectroscopy is another technique used for identification, either on the glaze surface or on a polished cross section. It is effective in identifying crystalline compounds associated with decorations or glazes and can also determine glaze components when direct sampling is not possible.

The colour of glass and glazes is primarily determined by the absorption of light in the visible wavelength range. Absorption is influenced by the presence of various ions, particularly transition metal ions. *UV-Vis-NIR spectroscopy* is the most accessible technique for chromophore identification, with the exact position of the absorption bands depending on the chromophore groups and glass components. Colour analysis can be performed using an Ulbricht Sphere

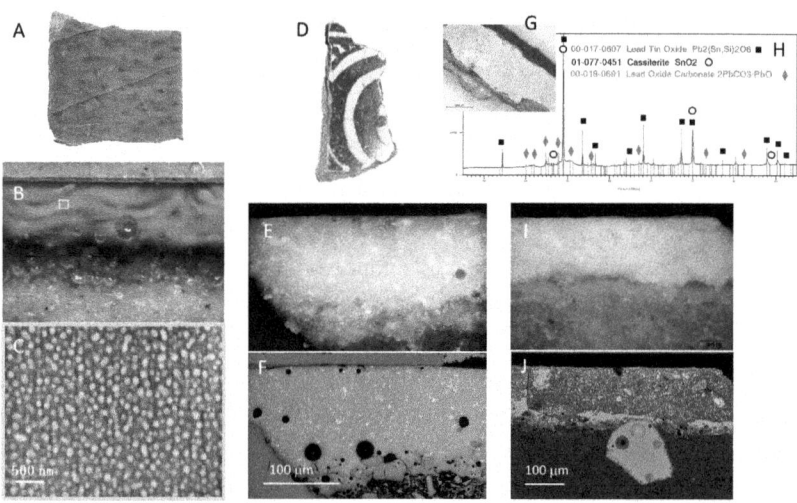

Figure 11 Images of the different glazed ceramic fragments and the corresponding cross sections. (A–C) Jun ware from the Northern Song dynasty, 13th century (J24) (Yuan et al. 2022). (D–F) Lustre painted Fatimid ware from Egypt, 11th century (P169) (Pradell et al. 2008). (G-J) Yellow glazed ware found at Madīnat al-Zahrā palace, Cordoba Caliphate, 10th century (MZ2) (Salinas et al. 2019), h is the XRD pattern of glaze.

and a double-beam spectrometer, allowing the determination of colour coordinates in the CIELAB colour model.

X-ray Absorption Near Edge Structure (XANES) and *Extended X-ray Absorption Fine Structure* (EXAFS) are synchrotron-based techniques that allow for precise analysis of oxidation states and coordination sites by scanning X-rays around the absorption band of an element. *XANES* focuses on the absorption edge, while *EXAFS* extends the spectral range to analyse interference between scattered X-rays, providing information about the atoms in the first coordination sphere. These techniques can be used in combination with *XRF* on glaze surfaces or polished cross sections, providing quantitative and non-invasive analysis, although sample manipulation is required to access different areas of the glaze. Again, beam penetration is key as the first few tens of microns of the glaze surface are more susceptible to the atmosphere during cooling and also to alteration than the inner areas. It is therefore preferable to work on cross sections with a micro-beam.

6.3 Main Glaze Components

6.3.1 Chemical Composition of the Glaze

Glazes are composed of three main components: silica, alumina, and a flux. Silica is the main glass former, alumina provides stability and prevents excessive flow, and a flux is an element that lowers the melting point of the glaze and helps it adhere to the ceramic body. Glazes may also contain various additives, such as colourants, opacifiers, and modifiers, to achieve different aesthetic and technical results.[4] Glazes can be classified according to their firing temperature, which affects their composition and properties. Low-temperature glazes are fired at temperatures between 900°C and 1050°C, while high-temperature glazes are fired at temperatures above 1100°C. The fluxes of low temperature glazes are lead, sodium, and potassium oxides, while the fluxes of high-temperature glazes are calcium, sodium, and potassium oxides. Frits are pre-melted glaze ingredients that are ground into a powder and mixed with water before they are applied to the ceramic.

Amorphous Phase

The amorphous phase may be the only component in a transparent glaze or a minor component in some opaque or underfired glazes. The amorphous phase is the solid melt, and its composition depends on the raw materials of the glaze and also on the interaction with the ceramic body during firing; see Figure 9.

The interaction between the glaze and ceramic body leads to the dissolution of some ceramic components in the glaze and interdiffusion of elements

---

[4] https://link.springer.com/article/10.1007/s12520-020-01136-9

between them. As a result, the glazes exhibit non-homogeneity, with chemical composition gradients present across the thickness of the glaze due to the process of diffusion (Molera et al. 2001). The incorporation of ceramic elements into the glaze alters its chemistry, and it is obvious that the thinner the glaze, the more the chemical composition is affected. It also depends on the materials and the method of application of the glaze. Glaze mixtures can be applied directly to raw ceramic (single firing) or to pre-fired ceramic (double firing), the former incorporating more elements into the glaze than the latter. Fluxes can be of different types: vegetable ash, alkaline and alkaline earth carbonates, lead oxide, lead sulphide. They can also be used alone or mixed with sand (quartz sand with or without feldspar). Finally, the glazes can be pre-fired (fritted) or applied directly. Consequently, the final composition and microstructure of the glazes are also greatly influenced by the method of glaze application. In some cases, it is possible to identify the materials and method of application; in others it is not. For instance, in the case of lead glazes, by comparing the SiO_2 and Al_2O_3 content of the ceramic and glaze, after excluding the contribution of lead oxide and colourants and normalizing, it is possible to determine whether a mixture of lead oxide, PbO, and quartz, SiO_2, or lead oxide alone was used (Walton et al. 2010).

Due to the interaction of the ceramic with the glaze, glazes show an interface, they also show undissolved or relic particles, new crystalline compounds, bubbles from the decomposition of the raw compounds. It is also common to see cracks due to the different shrinkage of glaze and ceramic during the cooling, or to alteration. Corrosion products are also often precipitated inside cracks, bubbles, along the interface or deposited on the surface as is shown in Figure 9.

Interface

The interaction between the glaze and the ceramic body alters the chemistry of the glazes, particularly at the glaze-ceramic interface, often resulting in the formation of crystalline compounds at the interface; see Figure 9. The composition and nature of these crystals depend on the firing temperature and the composition of the ceramic and the glaze. Lead-potassium feldspars, $(Pb,K)AlSi_3O_8$, are formed in lead glazes (Molera et al. 1993); both lead and alkali glazes on calcareous ceramics lead to the formation of feldspars (plagioclases), wollastonite ($CaSiO_3$), and on a calcium and magnesium rich ceramic to pyroxenes $(Mg,Ca,Fe,Al)_2Si_2O_6$ (Pradell et al. 2010).

Some studies have suggested a correlation between the thickness of the reaction layer and both the application of the glaze to the raw or fired ceramic substrate and the firing temperature (Tite et al. 1998). However, although they are probably the most important, the glaze thickness, firing protocol (time/temperature), and ceramic composition can also influence the formation of a thicker or thinner interaction layer (Molera et al. 2001; Pradell et al. 2013).

6.3.2 Opacifiers

Transparency in ceramic glazes is not always desirable, as the colour of the underlying ceramic body (from buff colour to red or black) can interfere with the colour of the glaze and decorative motifs. Applying a white slip or the bleaching of the ceramic surface were common early methods of avoiding this, but the production of opaque glazes was soon adopted. Opacity in glazes can be achieved by the generation of a large number of bubbles, by the presence of undissolved quartz or feldspar particles, or by the presence of small precipitates (about 1 μm) of cassiterite, SnO_2, wollastonite, pyroxene or feldspar, dispersed in the glaze, or, as mentioned earlier, precipitate at the glaze-ceramic interface, with net crystalline surface which scatter light more efficiently increasing the opacity (Figure 11). Large bubbles and undissolved particles produce a partially opaque glaze, while the small crystallites formed during the glaze firing with neat crystalline surfaces and a high refractive index further increase the opacity. In particular, the addition of an excess of quartz particles to the glaze mixture results in a glaze full of undissolved quartz particles which act as a white opacifier (Figure 12). This method has been used in particular in those periods and regions (9th- and 10th-century Sicily and North Africa) (Salinas et al. 2020; Salinas et al. 2022) that did not have other opacifiers, in particular, as we will see next, tin. Tin is not as common as lead, and it is known to have been traded from remote regions (Uzbekistan, England) to the Mediterranean production centres.

When a mixture of PbO, SnO_2 and SiO_2 is fired together, it undergoes several transformations resulting in the formation of yellow lead-tin oxide (Pb_2SnO_4) particles, which then transform to $(Pb,Si)_2Sn_2O_6$ particles at higher temperatures, and finally dissolve in the melt to recrystallize as well shaped SnO_2 particles, usually less than one micron in size. The temperatures at which these transformations occur depend on the composition of the mixture, with higher PbO/SiO_2 ratios resulting in more stable $(Pb,Si)_2Sn_2O_6$ particles. Therefore, yellow glazes typically have a high PbO/SiO_2 ratio (typically 62–68% PbO and 24–30% SiO_2) (Figure 11 G-J) (Molera et al. 1999; Tite, et al. 2008; Tite et al. 2015). In order to decrease the lead content, plant ashes were added in the white glazes to reduce the PbO content and increase other fluxes as Na, K and Ca (Figure 11 D-F; Matin et al. 2018).

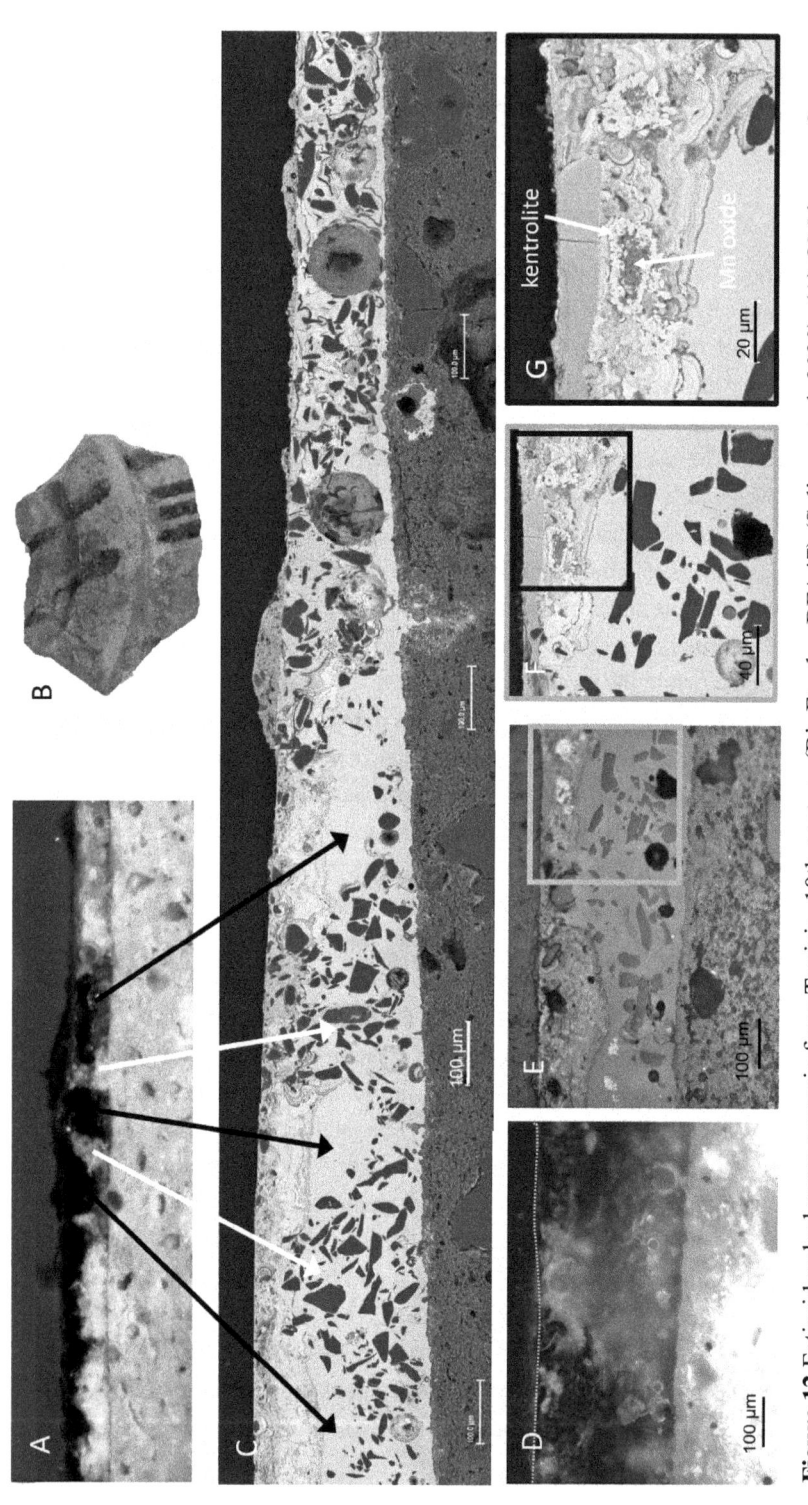

Figure 12 Fatimid polychrome ceramic from Tunisia, 10th century (Bir Ftouha, BFA47) (Salinas et al. 2020), (A) OM image of a cross section of an overglaze brown decoration. (B) Image of the fragment. (C) BSD image of the same cross section. (D) Dark-field and (E) bright-field OM images of an enlarged area. (F) Enlarged area of E. (G) Enlarged area of F.

Tin dissolves in alkaline glazes, but can appear precipitate at the glaze-ceramic interface as a calcium tin silicate, malayaite, CaSn(SiO4)O (Tite et al. 2002). However, as a reaction compound, it is not uncommon in copper glasses and glazes, as tin is a common impurity associated with copper. Similarly, brizziite, NaSbO3, has also been found in some alkaline glasses and glazes when antimony is present (Amadori et al. 2023).

Opacity can also be achieved in lime glazes (high temperature) when the SiO_2/Al_2O_3 ratio is high (above 6–7). In this case, the high temperature immiscibility between a lime-rich glass and a silica-rich glass results in a glaze nanostructure. Typical structures are lime-rich droplets in a silica-rich matrix, or silica-rich droplets in a lime-rich matrix, or mixed nano-structures (Figure 11A-C). Light scattering of these structures is responsible for the opacity of the glazes. In modern times (19th century) titanium oxide has replaced tin oxide as a white opacifier.

6.3.3 Colourants and Decorations

Colour is usually added to glazes by the addition of metal cations, among which the most common are Mn^{2+}, Mn^{3+}, Co^{2+}, Cu^{+}, Cu^{2+}, Fe^{3+}, and Fe^{2+}. Often, there is more than one present, and a balance is achieved between the different species present, which gives the glaze its characteristic colour. They can also appear in different site coordinations, four-, five-, or six-fold, and this also determines the colour of the glaze (Weyl 2016).

Metal cations can also react with the glaze components during the firing to form crystalline compounds. The reaction compounds formed depend on the composition of the glaze, the firing temperature, the atmosphere, and the concentration of the metal itself. Consequently, dissolved transition metal cations and crystalline precipitates are characteristic of the materials, method of application and firing process.

Colour can be applied to the entire glaze by mixing the colourants with the raw glaze, or decorative motifs can be painted. Decorations are particularly interesting because they can be made in a wide variety of ways: overglaze, underglaze, *enamel*, side-by-side, *cuerda seca*, with one or more firings. Depending on the process used different crystalline compounds are obtained, which appear heterogeneously distributed in the glaze. Underglaze painting is applied to a raw dry ceramic surface, followed by a first firing, and then the ceramic is glazed and subjected to a second firing (Figure 13). This allows finer designs to be drawn while the first firing fixes them and reduces blurring. Although it is also possible to use a single firing, the designs will be less defined. Overglaze decorations are painted directly over the raw glaze applied either over a biscuit or raw ceramic which is then fired (Figure 13). Painting over a raw glaze is more difficult which,

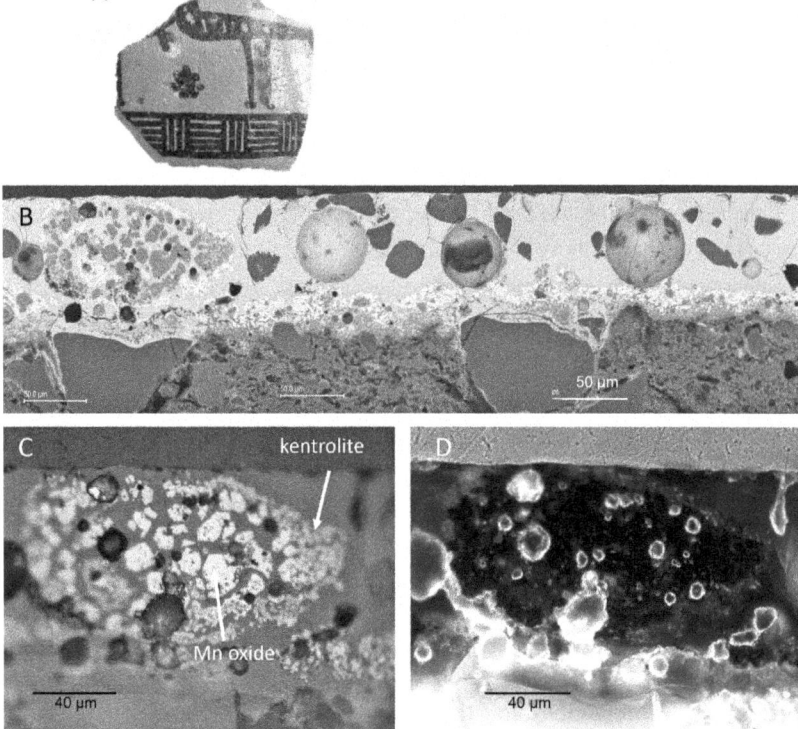

Figure 13 (A) Image of an Aglabid Raqqada type, polychrome ceramic from Tunisia, 9th century (CS66) (Salinas et al. 2020). (B) SEM BSD image of a cross section of the brown area. (C) Bright-field and (D) dark-field OM images of a detail of the brown decoration.

together with the diffusion of the metal cations, makes the designs less precise. The pigments are often mixed with some clay or raw glaze mixture to facilitate the reaction with the ceramic/glaze and to fix them. Side-by-side painting refers to the application of different coloured glazes directly over the ceramic surface. *Enamels* are a prepared mixture of glass with a pigment or colourant that is fired at a lower temperature onto the glazed object. This is very commonly used in porcelain and stoneware, less commonly, although not unknown, in low-temperature ceramics. Finally, the *cuerda seca*, a brown or black paint made from manganese and/or iron oxides mixed with a greasy compound, was used to delineate and separate the areas to be given different colours. The greasy compound spits out the colours, preventing them from mixing.

A detailed study of the reaction compounds and their distribution in the glaze gives direct information about the firing conditions (temperature and atmosphere) and the decoration method used.

Manganese

Manganese cations (Mn^{2+} and Mn^{3+}) and crystalline reactions compounds produce a range of colours depending on the glaze composition and temperature of firing, purple and blue colours in an alkaline glaze and purplish-brown and black colours in plumbic glazes. Extensive research has been carried out on the crystalline precipitates formed by the reaction between the manganese oxides with the lead glaze and ceramic as a function of the firing temperature (Molera et al. 2013; Molera et al. 2022). Barysilite, $(Pb,Mn)Si_2O_7$, is only expected in lead glazes fired at low temperatures below 850°C. Prismatic crystals of kentrolite, $Pb_2Mn_2Si_2O_9$, are formed above 700°C around bixbyite, Mn_2O_3, particles. Kentrolite crystals melt above 900°C and recrystallize on cooling with a different crystal habit (feathery instead of prismatic) (Figures 12 and 13), but only if a maximum temperature of 980°C is not reached. Braunite, Mn_7SiO_{12}, crystals are formed above 900°C and are stable up to 1020°C. The shape of braunite crystals varies from square shaped at 900°C to a dendritic morphology around 1000°C. However, these crystals will only form if there is enough manganese is present; otherwise, the manganese will dissolve completely in the glaze without forming crystals.

In lead glazes enriched with calcium, the sequence of crystalline phases formed is as follows: at low temperatures, ganomalite, $Pb_3(CaMn)_2Si_3O_{11}$, margarosanite, $Pb(Ca,Mn)_2Si_3O_9$, and kentrolite, above 850°C Mn-wollastonite, $(Mn,Ca)SiO_3$, followed at higher temperatures by bustamite, $(Mn,Ca)_3Si_3O_9$. In the presence of magnesium Mn-diopsides, $Ca(Mg,Mn)Si_2O_6$, are formed at all temperatures (Molera et al. 2022).

Iron

Iron has also been used as a pigment since ancient times. It can be added to the glaze to give colour, or it can be incorporated into the glaze by diffusion from the ceramic body. Depending on the atmosphere of the kiln, it gives different colours: in a reducing atmosphere, a blue colour due to the presence of Fe^{2+}, or in an oxidizing atmosphere, a yellow to amber colour depending on the concentration and thickness of the glaze due to the presence of Fe^{3+}. However, both Fe^{2+} and Fe^{3+} are normally present in the glazes giving green to brown colours depending on the concentration and their relative amount.

When a high concentration of iron oxide is present in lead glazes, barysilite, $Pb_8FeSi_2O_7$, and melanotekite $Pb_2Fe_2Si_2O_9$, are both formed below 650°C and melted below 700°C and 930°C, respectively. Melanotekite forms a complete solid solution with kentrolite and can incorporate Mn in its structure. However, melanotekite is less stable than kentrolite and melts below 930°C. At higher temperatures, only hematite and some cristobalite and quartz remain in lead glazes. The neoformed crystals of Fe_2O_3 have a platelet hexagonal shape (Di Febo et al. 2017) but with the presence of kaolinite in the mixture cubic-shaped hematite crystals are formed (Molera et al. 2025).

In the presence of calcium, andradite, $Ca_3Fe_2(SiO_4)_3$, crystals could be formed at 850°C and magnetoplumbite, $PbFe_{12}O_{19}$, at higher temperatures (980°C). In the presence of magnesium Fe-diopsides, $(Fe,Ca)MgSi_2O_6$, are formed at 750°C, and with the presence of manganese, jacobsite, $MnFe_2O_4$, is formed at 928°C (Molera et al. 2025).

Copper

Copper has a high diffusivity and tends to dissolve completely in the glaze. Copper, like iron, can contribute different colours to glazes. In oxidizing environments, both Cu^{2+} and Cu^+ ions are present. The broad and intense absorption of Cu^{2+} in the red (800 nm), extending towards yellow, together with variations in the coordination of neighbouring atoms, results in a spectrum of colours ranging from turquoise to green. When there is a high concentration of copper oxide, copper-rich pyroxene crystals precipitate, and, in exceptional cases, copper lead silicates may also form.

On the other hand, firing the glazes under reducing conditions can cause some copper ions to be reduced to cuprite, Cu_2O or even to the metallic state, $Cu°$. Cuprite, which shows characteristic dendritic growth, gives a yellow to orange colour to the glazes depending on the size of the crystals. On the contrary, metallic copper tends to form small crystals of nanometric dimensions which absorb and scatter light giving a dark-red colour (see 5.4 lustre).

Cobalt

Cobalt has been utilized since ancient times to impart a blue hue to glass and glazes. Cobalt tends to dissolve into the silica glaze and imparts a blue colour when Co^{2+} is surrounded by four oxygens (CoO_4), and a pink colour when it forms octahedral coordination with six oxygens

The presence of arsenic in blue-decorated glazes, specifically observed in Europe from around 1520 onwards but absent prior to that, could be attributed to the ore processing methods employed. This includes the roasting of cobalt arsenide, the addition of sand and potash (smalt) to create glass, and the utilization of by-products from other metallurgical processes like silver smelting slag. Roasting cobalt arsenide ore alone or in combination with fluxes like PbO or CaF_2, $CaCO_3$, SiO_2, and kaolinite is insufficient to eliminate arsenic completely. Calcium arsenates, lead arsenates ($Pb_5(AsO_4)_3$ F, $Pb_8As_2O_{13}$), and calcium lead arsenates $(Ca,Pb)_5(AsO_4)_3(F,Cl,OH)$ with a hedyphane structure (Molera et al. 2021) are common crystals found in blue decorated glazes from 1500 onwards. Co is dissolved into the glassy matrix, but Co-Fe-Ni spinels could also be found in dense blue decorations. Cobalt aluminates have also been found in the underglaze blue decorated Chinese porcelain due to the high temperatures reached.

6.4 Lustre

Lustre (Caiger-Smith 1985; Pradell 2016) is a decoration constituted by a thin layer of metallic nanoparticles composed of silver and/or copper beneath the glaze surface. It exhibits a wide range of colours (green, yellow, amber, red, brown, white), metallic-like (golden, coppery, silvery) and iridescent (bluish, purplish) appearances (Pradell et al. 2012). The process involves applying a lustre pigment mixed with tin/lead calx and gum arabic (later substituted with an iron oxide and clay mixture) over the glaze surface and firing it at relatively low temperatures (Pradell 2016). The reaction between the silver and copper compounds in the lustre paint and the sodium and potassium ions in the glaze surface occurs through an 'ionic exchange' mechanism (Pradell et al. 2005; Molera et al. 2007). Reduction gases produced during firing, as well as the addition of reducing agents, facilitate the reduction of silver and copper ions to a metallic state and the formation of a thin layer of metallic nanoparticles. The colour, reflectivity, and iridescences shown by lustre layers made are due to the nature (copper, cuprite and/ or silver) and volume fraction of the nanoparticles, the presence of metal cations (Cu^+, Cu^{2+} and/or Ag^+), and the thickness of the layer (from 0.5 micrometres to some tens of micrometres).

6.5 Conclusions

The investigation of glazes offers valuable insights into the techniques and expertise of potters, enabling the identification of similar decorations created using different methods. By analysing the composition of the glass, examining the microstructure, and studying the crystalline phases, we can not only determine firing protocols but also uncover connections between communities and understand the transmission of knowledge. This wealth of information contributes to a deeper understanding of historical ceramics and the cultural exchange surrounding their production.

7 Further Surface Treatments

Anno Hein

7.1 Surface Treatments

Apart from silicate glazes there is a large variety of other and more rudimental techniques for finishing ceramic surfaces. After the moulding, the surfaces of the not yet dried vessels are commonly finished by smoothening or brushing. Warps and striations are flattened either by hand or by using tools extracting at the same time near-surface non-plastic particles (Roux 2019). In the further manufacturing process the internal and external surfaces of the vessels are often remoistened and burnished by applying friction. Through burnishing the superficial layer is compacted and the clay particles are aligned parallel to the surface (Ionescu & Hoeck 2020). Alternatively, or in addition, the ceramic surface can be coated with various materials either before firing or after firing. The scope of the coating can be decoration or the improvement of the properties of the surface for example in view of hardness or impermeability. The pre-firing coating with silicate rich material vitrifying during the firing has been discussed earlier. Other common coating materials are organic and carbonaceous materials as well as clay based slurries (Roux 2019). A clay-rich material in liquid state can be applied as a slip on the wet to bone hard vessel surface, for example, by dipping the entire vessel into a clay water mixture or by painting (Velde & Druc 1999). The slip can be produced from the initial clay paste used for the vessel manufacture by further refining commonly through elutriation and thus extracting the sand and silt fraction. Alternatively, an independent raw material naturally rich in clay minerals can be used as slip. During the firing process the clay-rich surface layer is vitrifying more extensively compared to the ceramic bodyenhancing the abrasion resistance of the surface (Skibo et al. 1997) and reducing its permeability (Schiffer 1990). The slip material can be enriched with components, such as metal oxides or pigments, inducing particular colours on the surface during firing (Noll et al. 1975). Organic coatings, such as resin, beeswax, oil, or milk, can be applied before firing or more commonly after firing on the still hot surface in order to impregnate it (Drieu et al. 2020; Rueff et al. 2021). Alternatively, the pottery surface or rather its pores can be smudged with pyrolized organic matter during the firing (Schiffer et al. 1994). Another common surface treatment apart from coating is the texturing by impression, incision, or stamping (Roux 2019). The texture might have a primarily decorative scope, but through enlarging of the surface area, the thermal properties of the vessel, such as its heating efficiency, are enhanced (Schiffer 1990; Schiffer et al. 1994).

7.2 Analytical Examination of the Surface

For the investigation of surface finishing essentially the same analytical techniques can be applied for analysing silicate glazes discussed already. An initial visual inspection with or without a microscope allows for assessing texture and roughness distinguishing, for example, between plain smoothening and burnishing based on the reflection of light. The relief and texture of decorated surfaces can be recorded, for example, using reflectance transformation imaging (RTI) or 3D laser scanning confocal microscopy (Artal-Isbrand & Klausmeyer 2013). In the case of RTI, series of digital images are taken using different angles of illumination and combined to an interactive map of the surface topography. In the case of laser scanning confocal microscopy a sequence of sections of the surface at increasing height is scanned and combined to an elevation map. Alternatively, optical interferometry can be applied for investigating roughness and surface topography at micrometre level through vertical scanning interferometry (VSI) (Ionescu et al. 2019). Elemental analysis of surface layers can indicate clay-rich slips or paints based on the enrichment or depletion of specific elements in comparison to the ceramic body. For this, the surfaces of vessels or fragments can be analysed with non-invasive or minimally invasive methods, such as pXRF, PIXE, or LA-ICP-MS (Chaviara & Aloupi-Siotis 2016; Shoval & Gilboa 2016; Shoval 2017; Sciau et al. 2020). In the case that it is possible to take samples these can be examined under the SEM. The examination of sections allows for examining the micro-stratigraphy of surface layers and their micromorphology in terms of degree of vitrification and granulometry (Sciau et al. 2020). Furthermore, the elemental composition of body and surface layers can be determined using SEM-EDS or EMPA (Aloupi-Siotis 2020). The top-view examination of the surface under the SEM in high magnification allows for further examining the surface texture in view of different finishing techniques (Ionescu & Hoeck 2020). For the supplementary examination of the mineralogical composition of the surface layers, micro XRD and Raman microscopy can be applied (Scarpelli et al. 2014; Aloupi-Siotis 2020; Sciau et al. 2020). In view of iron-based coatings and the reconstruction of the firing process the oxidation state of the iron compounds is of particular interest, which can be investigated with near-edge X-ray absorption spectroscopy (XAS) (Gliozzo et al. 2004; Aloupi-Siotis 2020). The analytical study of organic coatings on surfaces of archaeological ceramics is comparably complex and ambiguous as, for example, in the case of cooking pots intentional coating during manufacture and organic residues due to use cannot be clearly distinguished (Drieu et al. 2020). The research is often based on the examination of experimental coating in controlled laboratory conditions (Schiffer et al. 1994; Rueff et al. 2021). For the investigation of archaeological ceramics surface layers can be studied in sections under the optical microscope. Furthermore, the molecular composition of the organic compounds in the ceramic surface can be analysed with gas chromatography–mass spectrometry (GC/MS) (Drieu et al. 2020).

8 Statistical Approaches to the Evaluation of Analytical Data in Ceramic Studies

Anno Hein

Pottery vessels or fragments discovered in archaeological excavations represent up to a large extent the original composition and microstructure of the ceramics. As discussed in the previous sections, the analytical examination of these finds provides information about various aspects of the ceramics, such as manufacturing technology, chronology, provenance, or use and function. The study of technology concerns the investigation of raw material selection and processing, design and forming of the vessels, surface finishing, firing technology, and, eventually, the functionality of the final product. The study of ceramic provenance, on the other hand, allows for investigating trade networks based on the dissemination of specific ceramic wares as well as cultural networks based on preferences in terms of vessel design and decoration and the observed technology transfer. Commonly, ceramic objects, in contrast to other Cultural Heritage items, are not considered as singular or unique cases but rather as representatives of categories. For this, a typical analytical ceramic study includes the examination of a sufficient number of cases, the definition of categories based on the collected data, and the categorization of the cases. The categories can be defined based on different criteria depending on the analytical approach applied, such as elemental or mineralogical composition, petrographic fabric, chronology, decoration, or vessel type. For an initial categorization the frequency distribution of individual parameters can be graphically investigated with bar diagrams, pie diagrams, or scatter plots, while for the concurrent consideration of multiple parameters multivariate statistical methods are essential. It has to be considered, though, that categories according to different criteria do not necessarily coincide. Ceramics belonging to a specific petrographic fabric group, for example, might present diverse elemental compositions, or, on the other hand, different fabric groups might show similar trace element compositions. For this, an integrated study of a ceramic assemblage combining different analytical techniques as well as archaeological classification is expected to provide an integral picture by exploiting and assembling complementary information (Day et al. 1999).

8.1 Data Types

Concerning the treatment of the collected data, different types of data have to be distinguished (Papageorgiou 2020). In the initial state of an examination raw data are recorded, which can be digital, such as spectra, images, measured curves or time series, or analogue, such as photographs, drawings, or even

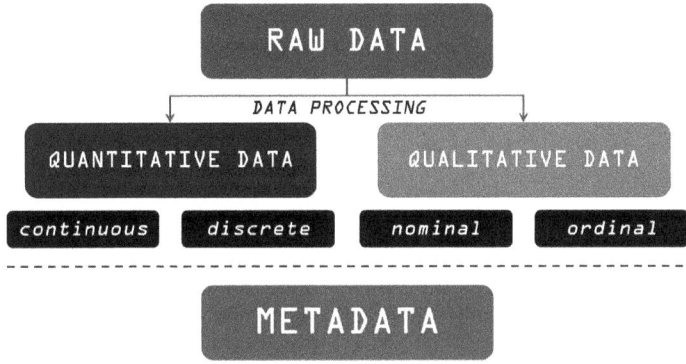

Figure 14 Different types of data, which can be collected and evaluated

notes. These raw data are commonly processed in order to obtain either quantitative data or qualitative data, which can be further statistically evaluated in order to define categories of similar cases. Quantitative or numerical data again can be distinguished in continuous data, such as elemental concentrations, content of particular minerals or specific material properties, and discrete data, such as the number of specific features. The qualitative or categorical data, on the other hand, can be distinguished in nominal data, such as vessel type, colour, or petrographic feature, and ordinal data, which can be set in an order, such as coarseness or the degree of vitrification (Figure 14). Eventually, another essential part of the data concerns the metadata, which are data describing the other data and setting them into context.

8.2 Data Analysis

The types of the available data have to be considered for planning their evaluation. While for pattern recognition of non-processed raw data, such as images, the application of machine learning approaches becomes increasingly common (Fiorucci et al. 2020), processed quantitative and qualitative data still commonly are evaluated rather by using multivariate statistics. The results of a quantitative study of an assemblage is typically a $p \times n$ data matrix with p the number of cases or samples analysed and n the number of features or parameters measured, such as the concentrations of individual elements. In archaeological science the most common approach for examining such a multivariate data set is exploratory data analysis using, for example, hierarchical cluster analysis or principal component analysis (PCA). The scope of an exploratory data analysis is to transform the data to a form with reduced dimensions, which can be further examined for its structure (Baxter 2001). For this, the data have to be scaled or normalized in order to assess similarities or dissimilarities between data records of individual cases. Model-based approaches, on the other hand, postulate a data model, such as a multivariate normal distribution (MVN) for the elemental composition of a single case or of cases belonging to the same category (Papageorgiou 2020). An individual category is defined by a reference pattern $x = (x_1, x_2, ..., x_n)$ comprising the mean values of the features estimated with the average values measured of representative cases (Hein & Kilikoglou 2017). The variability of the reference pattern is estimated by determining either the standard deviations of the features measured or the covariance matrix S_x (Baxter 2001). The margin of error of the mean values as well as of their variation depends on the number of cases included (Ahn & Fessler 2003). Taking into account S_x the similarity or dissimilarity of quantitative patterns of different categories or of an individual case with selected categories can be assessed with the Mahalanobis distance (Baxter 2001). Alternatively, only the diagonal terms of the covariance matrix are considered providing basically a weighted Euclidian distance (Hein & Kilikoglou 2017). Occasionally, a best relative fit is used in order to adjust the absolute values of the data records, which might be affected, for example, by different portions of non-plastic temper (Beier & Mommsen 1994). The variation matrix, which is based on the variances of the logarithmized ratios of the measured features, provides an alternative approach for assessing and treating the variability of a data set taking into consideration multivariate log-normal distributions (Buxeda i Garrigos 1999; Martín-Fernández et al. 2015). In the case of categorical data, possibly combined with quantitative data, different approaches have to be applied for assessing similarity or dissimilarity among data records. A common method applied to cross tables with two categorical variables is correspondence analysis (CA), which can be considered as PCA of nominal data. In a multiple correspondence analysis (MCA) three or more features are combined as columns in a matrix, in which the rows represent the examined cases (Cau et al. 2004). Furthermore, multidimensional scaling (MDS) can be applied, which, however, appears to be more suitable for examining ordinal categorical features. These allow also for measuring dissimilarities rather than testing only for concordance or discordance of specific features as in the case of nominal data (Angourakis et al. 2018). The quantitative and qualitative data collected in an integrated ceramic study eventually can be combined for multivariate evaluation in mixed-mode data analysis (Baxter et al. 2008; Angourakis et al. 2018).

References

Ahn, S. & Fessler, J. A. (2003). Standard errors of mean, variance and standard deviation estimators, Technical Report 413, Communications and Signal Processing Laboratory, University of Michigan.

Aidona, E., Polymeris, G., Camps, P. et al. (2018). Archaeomagnetic versus luminescence methods; the case of an early Byzantine ceramic workshop in Thessaloniki, Greece. *Arch.Anthropol.Sci.*, **10**, 725–741. https://doi.org/10.1007/s12520-017-0494-5.

Aidona, E., Spassov, S., Kondopoulou, D. et al. (2021). Archaeomagnetism and luminescence on medieval kilns in Thessaloniki and Chalkidiki (N. Greece): Implications for geomagnetic field variations during the last two millennia. *Phys.Earth.Planet.*, **316**, 106709. https://doi.org/10.1016/j.pepi.2021.106709.

Aitken, M. J. (1985). *Thermoluminescence Dating*. London: Academic Press.

Aitken, M. J. (1990). *Science-Based Dating in Archaeology*. London: Longman Press House.

Allegretta, I., Eramo, G., Pinto, D. & Hein, A. (2014). The effect of temper on the thermal conductivity of traditional ceramics: Nature, percentage and granulometry. *Thermochim.Acta*, **581**, 100–109. https://doi.org/10.1016/j.tca.2014.02.024.

Allegretta, I., Eramo, G., Pinto, D. & Kilikoglou, V. (2015). Strength of kaolinite-based ceramics: Comparison between limestone- and quartz-tempered bodies. *Appl.ClaySci.*, **116–117**, 220–230. https://doi.org/10.1016/j.clay.2015.03.018.

Aloupi-Siotis, E. (2020). Ceramic technology: How to characterise black Fe-based glass-ceramic coatings. *Archaeol.Anthropol.Sci.*, **12**, 191. https://doi.org/10.1007/s12520-020-01134-x.

Amadori, M. L., Matin, E., Poldi, G. et al. (2023). Archaeometric research on decorated bricks of Tol-e Ajori monumental gate (6th century BC), Fars, Iran: New insight into the glazes. *J.Cult.Herit.*, **60**, 63–71. https://doi.org/10.1016/j.culher.2023.01.005.

Amicone, S. R., Radivojevicć, M., Quinn, P. S., Berthold, C. & Rehren, T. (2020). Pyrotechnological connections: Pottery firing technology and the origins of metallurgy in the Vinca Culture, Serbia. *JAS*, **118**, 105123.

Angourakis, A., Martínez Ferreras, V., Torrano, A. & Gurt Esparraguera J. M. (2018). Presenting multivariate statistical protocols in reusing Roman wine amphorae productions in Catalonia, Spain. *JAS*, **93**, 150–165. https://doi.org/10.1016/j.jas.2018.03.007.

Aprile, A., Castellano, G. & Eramo, G. (2019). Classification of mineral inclusions in ancient ceramics: Comparing different modal analysis strategies. *Archaeol.Anthropol.Scis*, **11**, 2557–2567. https://doi.org/10.1007/s12520-018-0690-y.

Arnold, D. E. (1985). *Ceramic Theory and Cultural Process*. Cambridge: Cambridge University Press.

Artal-Isbrand, P. & Klausmeyer, P. (2013). Evaluation of the relief line and the contourline on Greek red-figure vases using reflectance transformation imaging and three-dimensional laser scanning confocal microscopy. *Stud. Conserv.*, **58**(4), 338–359. https://doi.org/10.1179/2047058412Y.0000000077.

Ashby, M. F. (2013). *Materials and the Environment – Eco-informed Material Choice* (2nd Ed.). Amsterdam: Butterworth-Heinemann.

Bailiff, I. K. (1994). The pre-dose technique. *Radiat.Meas.*, **23**, 471–479. https://doi.org/10.1016/1350-4487(94)90081-7.

Barnes, S. (1991). Electron microscopy and analysis at the Natural History Museum. *Microsc.Anal.*, **25**, 29–37.

Barone, G., Di Bella, M., Mastelloni, M. A. et al. (2017). Pigments characterization of polychrome vases production at Lipára: New insights by noninvasive spectroscopic methods. *X-RaySpectrom.*, **47**(1), 46–57. https://doi.org/10.1002/xrs.2810.

Baxter, M. J. (2001). Statistical modelling of artefact compositional data. *Archaeometry*, **43**(1), 131–147. https://doi.org/10.1111/1475-4754.00008.

Baxter, M. J. (2015). *Exploratory Multivariate Analysis in Archaeology, Foundations of Archaeology* (2nd Ed.). Clinton Corners, NY: Eliot Werner.

Baxter, M. J., Beardah, C. C., Papageorgiou, I. et al. (2008). On statistical approaches to the study of ceramic artefacts using geochemical and petrographic data. *Archaeometry*, **50**(1), 142–157. https://doi.org/10.1111/j.1475-4754.2007.00359.x.

Beckhoff, B., Kanngießer, B., Langhoff, N., Wedell, R. & Wolff, H. (2006). *Handbook of Practical X-Ray Fluorescence Analysis*. Heidelberg: Springer-Verlag.

Beier, T. & Mommsen, H. (1994). Modified Mahalanobis filters for grouping pottery by chemical composition. *Archaeometry*, **36**, 287–306. https://doi.org/10.1111/j.1475-4754.1994.tb00971.x.

Berg, I. (2008). Looking through pots: Recent advances in ceramics X-radiography. *JAS*, **35**, 1177–1188. https://doi.org/10.1016/j.jas.2007.08.006.

Bergaya, F. & Lagaly, G. (2006). General introduction: Clays, clay minerals and clay science. In Bergaya, F., Theng, B. K. G. & Lagaly, G., eds., *Handbook of Clay Science*. Amsterdam: Elsevier, pp. 1–18.

Betina, L. (2019). Contemporary pottery-making in Rhodes: Approaching ancient through modern craft traditions. *JASRep.*, **27**, 102003. https://doi.org/10.1016/j.jasrep.2019.102003.

Braekmans, D. & Degryse, P. (2017). Petrography: Optical microscopy. In Hunt, A., ed., *The Oxford Handbook of Archaeological Ceramic Analysis*. Oxford: Oxford University Press, pp. 233–265.

Bronitsky, G. & Hamer, R. (1986). Experiments in ceramic technology: The effects of various tempering materials on impact and thermal-shock resistance. *Am.Antiq.*, **51**, 89–101. https://doi.org/10.2307/280396.

Bruni, S., Longoni, M., De Filippi, F., Calore, N. & Bagnasco Gianni, G. (2023). External reflection FTIR spectroscopy applied to archaeological pottery: A non-invasive investigation about provenance and firing temperature. *Minerals*, **13**(9), 1211. https://doi.org/10.3390/min13091211.

Budja, M. (2011). Ceramic trajectories: From figurines to vessels. In Jordan P. & Zvelebil M., eds., *Ceramics before Farming: The Dispersal of Pottery among Prehistoric Eurasian Hunter-Gatherers*. Walnut Creek: Left Coast Press, pp. 499–525.

Burger, M., Glaus, R., Hubert, V. et al. (2017). Novel sampling techniques for trace element quantification in ancient copper artifacts using laser ablation inductively coupled plasma mass spectrometry. *JAS*, **82**, 62–71. https://doi.org/10.1016/j.jas.2017.04.009.

Burnstock, A. & Jones, C. (2000). Scanning electron microscopy techniques for imaging materials from paintings. In Creagh, D. C. & Bradley, D. A., eds., *Radiation in Art and Archaeometry*. Amsterdam: Elsevier, pp. 202–231.

Buxeda i Garrigos, J. (1999). Alteration and contamination of archaeological ceramics: The perturbation problem. *JAS*, **26**, 295–313. https://doi.org/10.1006/jasc.1998.0390.

Caiger-Smith, A. (1985). *Lustre Pottery: Technique, Tradition and Innovation in Islam and the Western World*. London: Faber and Faber.

Chaviara, A. & Aloupi-Siotis, E. (2016). The story of a soil that became a glaze: Chemical and microscopic fingerprints on the Attic vases. *JASRep.*, **7**, 510–518. https://doi.org/10.1016/j.jasrep.2015.08.016.

Cau, M. A., Day, P. M., Baxter, M. J. et al. (2004). Exploring automatic grouping procedures in ceramic petrology. *JAS*, **31**(9), 1325–1338. https://doi.org/10.1016/j.jas.2004.03.006.

Choleva, M. (2012). The first wheelmade pottery at Lerna: Wheel-thrown or wheel-fashioned? *Hesperia*, **81**(3), 343–381. https://doi.org/10.2972/hesperia.81.3.0343.

Courty, M. A. & Roux, V. (1995). Identification of wheel throwing on the basis of ceramic surface features and microfabrics. *JAS*, **22**, 17–50. https://doi.org/10.1016/S0305-4403(95)80161-8.

Cultrone, G., Rodriguez-Navarro, C., Sebastian, E., Cazalla, O. & De La Torre, M. J. (2001). Carbonate and silicate phase reactions during ceramic firing. *EJM*, **13**(3), 621–634. https://doi.org/10.1127/0935-1221/2001/0013-0621.

Day, P. M., Kiriatzi, E., Tsolakidou, A. & Kilikoglou, V. (1999). Group therapy in crete: A comparison between analyses by NAA and thin section petrography of Early Minoan Pottery, *JAS*, **26**, 1025–1036. https://doi.org/10.1006/jasc.1999.0424.

Demján, P., Pavúk. P. & Roosevelt, C. H. (2023). Laser-aided profile measurement and cluster analysis of ceramic shapes. *J.FieldArchaeol*, **48** (1), 1–18. https://doi.org/10.1080/00934690.2022.2128549.

Di Febo, R., Molera, J., Pradell, T., Vallcorba, O. & Capelli, C. (2017). Technological implications of neo-formed hematite crystals in ceramic lead glazes. *STAR*, **3** (2), International Symposium on Archaeometry 2016 (Kalamata, Greece): Proceedings. https://doi.org/10.1080/20548923.2017.1419675.

Donais, M. K. & George, D. B. (2018). *X-Ray Fluorescence Spectrometry and Its Applications to Archaeology: An Illustrated Guide*. New York: Momentum Press.

Drebushchak, V. A., Mylnikova L. N. & Molodin, V. I. (2007). Thermogravimetric investigation of ancient ceramics: Metrological analysis of sampling. *J.Therm. Anal.Calorim.*, **90**, 73–9. https://doi.org/10.1007/s10973-007-8478-9.

Drieu, L., Lepère, C. & Regert, M. (2020). The missing step of pottery chaîne opératoire: Considering post-firing treatments on ceramic vessels using macro- and microscopic observation and molecular analysis. *J.Archaeol. MethodTheory*, **27**, 302–326. https://doi.org/10.1007/s10816-019-09428-8.

Duller, G. A. T. (2008). *Luminescence Dating: Guidelines on Using Luminescence Dating in Archaeology*. Swindon: English Heritage.

Dussubieux, L., Golitko, M. & Gratuze, B. (2016). *Recent Advances in Laser Ablation ICP-MS for Archaeology*. Heidelberg: Springer Press.

Dussubieux, L., Golitko, M., Williams, P. R. & Speakman, J. (2007). Laser ablation-inductively coupled plasma-mass spectrometry analysis applied to the characterization of Peruvian Wari ceramics. In Glascock, M. D., Speakman, R. J. & Popelka-Filcoff, R. S., eds., *Archaeological Chemistry: Analytical Techniques and Archaeological Interpretation*. ACS Symposium Series **968**. Washington, DC: American Chemical Society, pp. 349–363.

Eckert, S. L. & James, W. D. (2011). Investigating the production and distribution of plain ware pottery in the Samoan archipelago with laser ablation-inductively coupled plasma-mass spectrometry (LA-ICP-MS). *JAS*, **38**, 2155–2170. https://doi.org/10.1016/j.jas.2011.03.009.

Edwards, H. G. M., Vandenabeele, P. & Colomban, P. (2023). *Raman Spectroscopy in Cultural Heritage Preservation*. Cham: Springer.

Fiorucci, M., Khoroshiltseva, M., Pontil, M. et al. (2020). Machine learning for cultural heritage: A survey. *Pattern Recognition Letters*, **133**, 102–108. https://doi.org/10.1016/j.patrec.2020.02.017.

Fleming, S. (1979). *Thermoluminescence Techniques in Archaeology*. Oxford: Clarendon Press.

Frahm, E. & Doonan, R. C. P. (2013). The technological versus methodological revolution of portable XRF in archaeology. *JAS*, **40**(2), 1425–1434. https://doi.org/10.1016/j.jas.2012.10.013.

Franklin, A. D., Prescott, J. R. & Scholefield, R. B. (1995). The mechanism of thermoluminescence in an Australian sedimentary quartz. *J.Lumin.*, **63**(5–6), 317–326. https://doi.org/10.1016/0022-2313(94)00068-N.

Froh, J. (2004). Archaeological ceramics studied by scanning electron microscopy. *Hyperfine.Interact.*, **154**, 159–176. https://doi.org/10.1023/B:HYPE.0000032074.98045.cc.

Gait, J., Bajnok, K., Szilágyi, V. et al. (2022). Quantitative 3D orientation analysis of particles and voids to differentiate hand-built pottery forming techniques using X-ray microtomography and neutron tomography. *Archaeol.Anthropol.Scis*, **14**, 223. https://doi.org/0.1007/s12520-022-01688-y.

Galli, A., Sibilia, E. & Martini, M. (2020). Ceramic chronology by luminescence dating: How and when it is possible to date ceramic artefacts. *Archaeol.Anthropol.Scis*, **12**, 190. https://doi.org/https://doi.org/10.1007/s12520-020-01140-z.

Gehres, B. & Querré, G. (2018). New applications of LA–ICP–MS for sourcing archaeological ceramics: Microanalysis of inclusions as fingerprints of their origin. *Archaeometry*, **60**(4), 750–763. https://doi.org/10.1111/arcm.12338.

Giussani, B., Monticelli, D. & Rampazzi, L. (2009). Role of laser ablation – inductively coupled plasma – mass spectrometry in cultural heritage research: A review. *Anal.Chim.Acta*, **635**, 6–21. https://doi.org/10.1016/j.aca.2008.12.040.

Glascock, M. D. (1992). Characterization of archaeological ceramics at MURR by neutron activation analysis and multivariate statistics. In Neff, H., eds., *Chemical Characterization of Ceramic Pastes in Archaeology*. Madison: Prehistory Press, pp. 11–26.

Glascock, M. D. & Neff, H. (2003). Neutron activation analysis and provenance research in archaeology. *Meas.Sci.Technol.*, **14**(9), 1516–1526. https://doi.org/10.1088/0957-0233/14/9/304.

Glaus, R., Koch, J. & Günther D. (2012). Portable laser ablation sampling device for elemental fingerprinting of objects outside the laboratory with laser ablation inductively coupled plasma mass spectrometry. *Anal.Chem.*, **84** (12), 5358–5364. https://doi.org/10.1021/ac3008626.

Gliozzo, E. (2020). Ceramic technology: How to reconstruct the firing process. *Archaeol.Anthropol.Scis*, **12**, 260. https://doi.org/10.1007/s12520-020-01133-y.

Gliozzo, E., Kirkman, I. W., Pantos, E. & Memmi Turbanti, I. (2004). Black gloss pottery: Production sites and technology in northern Etruria, part II: Gloss technology. *Archaeometry*, **46**, 227–246. https://doi.org/10.1111/j.1475-4754.2004.00154.x.

Göksu, H. Y., Wieser, A. & Regulla, D. F. (1989). 110°C TL peak records the ancient heat treatment of flint. *AncientTL*, **7**(1), 15–17. http://ancienttl.org/ATL_07-1_1989/ATL_07-1_Goksu_p15-17.pdf.

Golitko, M. & Dussubieux, L. (2017). Inductively coupled plasma-mass spectrometry (ICPMS) and laser ablation inductively coupled plasma-mass spectrometry (LA-ICP-MS). In Hunt, A., ed., *The Oxford Handbook of Archaeological Ceramic Analysis*. Oxford: Oxford University Press, pp. 399–423.

Gosselain, O. P. & Livingstone Smith, A. (2005). The source: Clay selection and processing practices in sub-Saharan Africa. In Livingstone Smith, A., Bosquet, D. & Martineau, R., eds., *Pottery Manufacturing Processes: Reconstitution and Interpretation*. BAR-IS 1349. Oxford: BAR, pp. 33–47.

Gratuze, B., Blet-Lemarquand, M. & Barrandon, J. N. (2001). Mass spectrometry with laser sampling: A new tool to characterize archaeological materials. *J.Radioanal.Nucl.Chem.*, **247**, 645–656. https://doi.org/10.1023/A:1010623703423.

Gualteri, S. (2020). Ceramic raw materials: How to establish the technological suitability of a raw material. *Archaeol.Anthropol.Scis*, **12**, 183. https://doi.org/10.1007/s12520-020-01135-w.

Hall, M. (2017). X-ray fluorescence-energy dispersive (ED-XRF) and wavelength dispersive (WD-XRF) spectrometry. In Hunt, A., eds., *The Oxford Handbook of Archaeological Ceramic Analysis*. New York: Oxford University Press, pp. 343–381.

Harbottle, G. (1976). Activation analysis in archaeology. In Newton, G. W. A., ed., *Radiochemistry 3*. London: The Chemical Society, pp. 33–72.

Hazenfratz-Marks, R. (2017). Evaluating data: Uncertainty in ceramic analysis. In Hunt, A., ed., *The Oxford Handbook of Archaeological Ceramic Analysis*. New York: Oxford University Press, pp. 386–409.

Heaney, P. J. (1994). Structure and chemistry of the low-pressure silica polimorphs. In Heaney P. J., Prewitt C. T. & Gibbs G. V., eds., *Silica. Physical Behavior, Geochemistry and Materials Applications*. Washington, DC: Mineralogical Society of America, pp. 1–40.

Heimann, R. (2017). X-ray powder diffraction (XRPD). In Hunt, A., ed., *The Oxford Handbook of Archaeological Ceramic Analysis*. New York: Oxford University Press, pp. 327–341.

Heimann, R. B. & Maggetti, M. (1981). Experiments on simulated burial of calcareous terra sigillata: Mineralogical changes – preliminary results. *BMOP*, **19**, 163–177.

Hein, A. & Kilikoglou, V. (2017). Compositional variability of archaeological ceramics in the Eastern Mediterranean and implications for the design of provenance studies. *JASRep*, **16**, 564–572. https://doi.org/10.1016/j.jasrep.2017.03.020.

Hein, A. & Kilikoglou, V. (2020a). Ceramic raw materials: How to recognize them and locate the supply basins: Chemistry. *Archaeol.Anthropol.Scis.*, **12**, 180. https://doi.org/10.1007/s12520-020-01129-8.

Hein, A. & Kilikoglou, V. (2020b). Digital modeling of function and performance of transport amphorae. *IJCES*, **2**, 187–200. https://doi.org/10.1002/ces2.10056.

Hein, A. & Kilikoglou, V. (2025). Modelling the material performance of ceramic vessels in view of their function and utilization. *Proceedings of the CAA 21*, Tübingen: Tübingen University Press.

Hein, A., Karatasios, I., Müller, N. S. & Kilikoglou, V. (2013). Heat transfer properties of pyrotechnical ceramics used in ancient metallurgy. *Thermochim.Acta*, **573**, 87–94. https://doi.org/10.1016/j.tca.2013.09.024.

Hein, A., Müller, N. S., Day, P. M. & Kilikoglou, V. (2008). Thermal conductivity of archaeological ceramics: The effect of inclusions, porosity and firing temperature. *Thermochim.Acta*, **480**, 35–42. https://doi.org/10.1016/j.tca.2008.09.012.

Hein, A., Vekinis, G. & Kilikoglou, V. (2022). Modeling of biaxial flexure tests of transport amphorae with the finite element method: Fracture strength, deformation and stress distribution. *RINENG*, **15**, 100508. https://doi.org/10.1016/j.rineng.2022.100508.

Hughes, T. J. R. (2000). *The Finite Element Method: Linear Static and Dynamic Finite Element Analysis*. New York: Dover.

Ionescu, C. & Hoeck, V. (2020). Ceramic technology: How to investigate surface finishing. *Archaeol.Anthropol.Sci*, **12**, 204. https://doi.org/10.1007/s12520-020-01144-9.

Ionescu, C., Fischer, C., Hoeck, V. & Lüttge, A. (2019). Discrimination of ceramic surface finishing by vertical scanning interferometry. *Archaeometry*, **61**(1), 31–42. https://doi.org/10.1111/arcm.12410.

Janssen, K. (2004). X-ray based methods of analysis. In Janssens, K. & Van Grieken, R., eds., *Non-destructive Microanalysis of Cultural Heritage Materials*. Compr.Anal.Chem.Series XLII. Amsterdam: Elsevier, pp. 129–226. https://doi.org/10.1016/S0166-526X(04)80008-4.

Jehlička, J. & Culka, A. (2022). Critical evaluation of portable Raman spectrometers: From rock outcrops and planetary analogs to cultural heritage – A review. *Anal.Chim.Acta*, **1209**, 339027. https://doi.org/10.1016/j.aca.2021.339027.

Jenkins, R. (1999). *X-Ray Fluorescence Spectrometry*. New York: Wiley.

Karasik, A. & Smilansky, U. (2008). 3D scanning technology as a standard archaeological tool for pottery analysis: Practice and theory. *JAS*, **35**, 1148–1168. https://doi.org/10.1016/j.jas.2007.08.008.

Karl, S., Jungblut, D., Mara, H., Wittum, G. & Krömker, S. (2014). Insights into manufacturing techniques of archaeological pottery: Industrial X-ray computed tomography as a tool in the examination of cultural material. In Martinón-Torres, M., ed., *Craft and Science: International Perspectives on Archaeological Ceramics*. Doha: Bloomsbury Qatar Foundation, pp. 253–261.

Käser, D. (2015). *Redesign of a portable laser ablation setup to allow sampling of ancient Chinese Jade and Porcelain* (Master Thesis), ETH Zürich. www.research-collection.ethz.ch/bitstream/handle/20.500.11850/189964/Masterthesis_DeboraK%C3%A4ser.pdf?sequence=1

Kennett, D. J., Sakai, S., Neff, H., Gossett, R. & Larson, D. O. (2002). Compositional characterization of prehistoric ceramics: A new approach. *JAS*, **29**(5), 443–455. https://doi.org/10.1006/jasc.2001.0737.

Kibaroğlu, M. & Thumm-Doğrayan, D. (2013). Trojan pithoi: A petrographic approach to provenance of Bronze Age storage vessels from Troy. *Appl. ClaySci.*, **82**, 44–52. https://doi.org/10.1016/j.clay.2013.06.023.

Kibaroğlu, M., Kozal, E., Klügel, A., Hartmann, G. & Monien, P. (2019). New evidence on the provenance of Red Lustrous Wheel-made Ware (RLW): Petrographic, elemental and Sr-Nd isotope analysis. *JASRep.*, **24**, 412–433. https://doi.org/10.1016/j.jasrep.2019.02.004.

Kibaroğlu, M., Sagona, A. & Satır, M. (2011). Petrographic and geochemical investigations of the Late Prehistoric ceramics from Sos Höyük, Erzurum

(Eastern Anatolia). *JAS*, **38**, 3072–3084. https://doi.org/10.1016/j.jas.2011.07.006.

Kibaroğlu, M., Satır, M. & Kastl, G. (2009). Petrographic and geochemical analysis on the provenance of the Middle Bronze and Late Bronze/Early Iron Age ceramics from Didi Gora and Udabno I, eastern Georgia. *JAS*, **36**, 2463–2474. https://doi.org/10.1016/j.jas.2009.07.005.

Kilikoglou, V., Vekinis, G., Maniatis, Y. & Day, P. M. (1998). Mechanical performance of quartz-tempered ceramics: Part I, strength and toughness. *Archaeometry*, **40**(2), 261–279. https://doi.org/10.1111/j.1475-4754.1998.tb00837.x.

Knaf, A. C. S., Koornneef, J. M. & Davies, G. R. (2017). 'Non-invasive' portable laser ablation sampling of art and archaeological materials with subsequent Sr–Nd isotope analysis by TIMS using 1013 Ω amplifiers. *J. Anal.At.Spectrom.*, **32**, 2210–2216. https://doi.org/10.1039/c7ja00191f.

Kontopoulou, D., Aidona, E., Ioannidis, N., Polymeris, G. S. & Tsolakis S. (2015). Archaeo-magnetic study and thermoluminescence dating of proto-byzantine kilos (Megali Kypsa, North Greece). *JASRep.*, **2**, 156–168. https://doi.org/10.1016/j.jasrep.2015.01.007.

Kosiba, S., Quave, K. E., Sharratt, N. et al. (2023). Local knowledge and imperial art: A preliminary LA-ICP-MS analysis of clay preference and ceramic production practices in ancient Cuzco (ca. 1100–1550 CE). *JASRep.*, **48**, 103870. https://doi.org/10.1016/j.jasrep.2023.103870.

Koul, D. K. (2006). Role of alkali ions in limiting the capacity of the 110°C peak of quartz to remember the firing temperature. *Appl.Radiat.Isot.*, **64**(1), 110–115. https://doi.org/10.1016/j.apradiso.2005.07.008.

Koul, D. K., Chougaonkar, M. P. & Polymeris, G. S. (2010). Applicability of OSL pre-dose phenomenon of quartz in the estimation of equivalent dose. *Radiat.Meas.*, **45**, 15–21. https://doi.org/10.1016/j.apradiso.2005.07.008.

Kozatsas, J., Kotsakis, K., Sagris, D. & David, K. (2018). Inside out: Assessing pottery forming techniques with micro-CT scanning. An example, from Middle Neolithic Thessaly. *JAS*, **100**, 102–119. https://doi.org/10.1016/j.jas.2018.10.007.

Kuzmin, Y. V. (2015). The origins of pottery in east Asia: Updated analysis (the 2015 state-of the art). *Doc.Preahist.*, **42**, 1–11. https://doi.org/10.4312/dp.42.1.

Liritzis, I. (2011). Surface dating by luminescence: An overview. *Geochronometria*, **38**(3), 292–302.

Liritzis, I., Aravantinos, V., Polymeris, G. S. et al. (2015). Witnessing prehistoric Delphi by Luminescence Dating. *Comptes.Rendus.Palevol*, **14**, 219–232.

Liritzis, I., Stamoulis, K., Papachristodoulou, Ch. & Ioannides, K. G. (2013). A re-evaluation of radiation dose rate conversion factors. *MAA*, **13**(3), 1–15.

Little, N. C., Kosakowsky, L. J., Speakman, R. J., Glascock, M. D. & Lohse, J. C. (2004). Characterization of Maya pottery by INAA and ICP-MS. *J.Radioanal. Nucl.Chem.*, **262**(1), 103–110. https://doi.org/10.1023/B:JRNC.0000040860.14672.89.

Llorca, J., González, C., Molina-Aldareguía, J. M. et al. (2011). Multiscale modeling of composite materials: A roadmap towards virtual testing. *Advanced Materials*, **23**, 5130–5147. https://doi.org/10.1002/adma.201101683.

Log, T. & Gustafsson, S. E. (1995). Transient Plane Source (TPS) Technique for measuring thermal transport: Properties of building materials. *Fire and Materials*, **19**, 43–49. https://doi.org/10.1002/fam.810190107.

Maggetti, M. (1982). Phase analysis and its significance for technology and origin. In Olin, J. S. & Franklin, A. D., eds., *Archaeological Ceramics*. Washington, DC: Smithsonian Institution Press, pp. 121–133.

Maggetti, M., Neururer, Ch. & Ramseyer, D. (2011). Temperature evolution inside a pot during experimental surface (bonfire) firing. *Appl.ClaySci.*, **53**, 500–508. https://doi.org/10.1016/j.clay.2010.09.013.

Mantler, M. & Schreiner, M. (2000). X-ray fluorescence spectrometry in art and archaeology. *X-RaySpectrom.*, **29**, 3–17. https://doi.org/10.1002/(SICI)1097-4539(200001/02)29:1<3::AID-XRS398>3.0.CO;2-O.

Maritan, L., Holakooei, P. & Mazzoli, C. (2015). Cluster analysis of XRPD data in ancient ceramics: What for? *Appl.ClaySci.*, **114**, 540–554. https://doi.org/10.1016/j.clay.2015.07.016.

Martín-Fernández, J. A., Buxeda i Garrigós J. & Pawlowsky-Glahn, V. (2015). Logratio analysis in archeometry: Principles and methods. In Barcelo, J. A. & Bogdanovic, I., eds., *Mathematics and Archaeology*. Boca Raton: CRC Press, pp. 178–189.

Matin, M., Tite, M. & Watson, O. (2018). On the origins of tin-opacified ceramic glazes: New evidence from early Islamic Egypt, the Levant, Mesopotamia, Iran, and Central Asia. *JASRep.*, **97**, 42–66. https://doi.org/10.1016/j.jas.2018.06.011.

Medeghini, L., Mignardi, S., Vito, C. et al. (2013). The key role of micro-Raman spectroscopy in the study of ancient pottery: The case of pre-classical Jordanian ceramics from the archaeological site of Khirbet al-Batrawy. *EJM*, **25**, 881–893. https://doi.org/10.1127/0935-1221/2013/0025-2332.

Molera, J., Bayes, C., Roura, P., Crespo, D. & Pradell, T. (2007). Key parameters in the production of medieval luster colors and shines. *JACerS*, **90**, 2245–2254. https://doi.org/10.1111/j.1551-2916.2007.01563.x.

Molera, J., Climent-Font, A., Garcia, G. et al. (2021). Experimental study of historical processing of cobalt arsenide ore for colouring glazes (15–16th century Europe). *JASRep.*, **36**, 10279. https://doi.org/10.1016/j.jasrep.2021.102797.

Molera, J., Coll, J., Labrador, A. & Pradell, T. (2013). Manganese brown decorations in 10th to 18th century Spanish tin glazed ceramics. *Appl. ClaySci.*, **82**, 86–90. https://doi.org/10.1016/j.clay.2013.05.018.

Molera, J., Colomer, M., Vallcorba, O. & Pradell, T. (2022). Manganese crystalline phases developed in high lead glazes during firing. *J.Eur.Ceram.Soc.*, **49**, 4006–4015. https://doi.org/10.1016/J.JEURCERAMSOC.2022.03.028.

Molera, J., Pradell, T., Martinez-Manent, S. & Vendrell-Saz, M. (1993). The growth of sanidine crystals in the lead of glazes of Hispano-Moresque pottery. *Appl.ClaySci.*, **7**, 483–491. https://doi.org/10.1016/0169-1317(93)90017-U.

Molera, J., Pradell, T., Salvado, N. & Vendrell-Saz, M. (1999). Evidence of tin oxide recrystallization in opacified lead glazes. *JACerS*, **82**, 2871–2875. https://doi.org/10.1111/j.1151-2916.1999.tb02170.x.

Molera, J., Pradell, T., Salvado, N. & Vendrell-Saz, M. (2001). Interactions between clay bodies and lead glazes. *JACerS*, **84**, 1120–1128. https://doi.org/10.1111/j.1151-2916.2001.tb00799.x.

Molera, J., Colomer, M., Vallcorba, O. & Pradell, T. (2025). Iron-manganese crystalline phases developed in high lead glazes during firing. *J.Eur.Ceram. Soc.*, **45**, 117244. https://doi.org/10.1016/j.jeurceramsoc.2025.117244.

Montana, G. (2020). Ceramic raw materials: How to recognize them and locate the supply basins – mineralogy, petrography. *Archaeol.Anthropol.Scis*, **12**, 180. https://doi.org/10.1007/s12520-020-01130-1.

Moon, D. H., Kim, S. J., Nam, S. W. & Cho, H. G. (2021). X-ray diffraction analysis of clay particles in ancient Baekje Black pottery: Indicator of the firing parameters. *Minerals*, **11**, 1239. https://doi.org/10.3390/min11111239.

Moropoulou, A., Bakolas, A. & Bisbikou, K. (1995). Thermal-analysis as a method of characterizing ancient ceramic technologies. *Thermochim. Acta*, **260**, 743–753. https://doi.org/10.1016/0040-6031(95)02570-7.

Müller, N. S., Hein, A., Georgakopoulou, M., Kilikoglou, V. & Kiriatzi, E. (2018). The effect of inter- and intra-source variation: A comparison between WDXRF and NAA data from Cretan clay deposits. *JASRep.*, **21**, 929–937. https://doi.org/10.1016/j.jasrep.2017.09.023.

Müller, N. S., Kilikoglou, V., Day, P. M. & Vekinis, G. (2010). The influence of temper shape on the mechanical properties of archaeological ceramics. *J.Eur. Ceram.Soc.*, **30**, 2457–2465. https://doi.org/10.1016/j.jeurceramsoc .2010.04.039.

Müller, N. S., Kilikoglou, V., Day, P. M. & Vekinis, G. (2014). Thermal shock resistance of tempered archaeological ceramics. In Martinón-Torres, M., ed., *Craft and Science: international Perspectives on Archaeological Ceramics*. Doha: Bloomsbury Qatar Foundation, pp. 263–270.

Müller, N. S., Vekinis, G., Day, P. M. & Kilikoglou, V. (2015). The influence of microstructure and texture on the mechanical properties of rock tempered archaeological ceramics. *J.Eur.Ceram.Soc.*, **35**, 831–843. https://doi.org/ 10.1016/j.jeurceramsoc.2014.09.025.

Müller, N. S., Vekinis, G. & Kilikoglou, V. (2016). Impact resistance of archaeological ceramics: The influence of firing and temper. *JASRep.*, **7**, 519–525. https://doi.org/10.1016/j.jasrep.2015.08.039.

Nakai, I. & Abe, Y. (2012). Portable X-ray powder diffractometer for the analysis of art and archaeological materials. *Appl.Phys.A*, **106**(2), 279–293. https://doi.org/10.1007/s00339-011-6694-4.

Neff, H. (2000). Neutron activation analysis for provenance determination in archaeology. In Ciliberto, E. & Spoto, G., eds., *Modern Analytical Methods in Art and Archaeology*. New York: Wiley, pp. 81–134.

Nelson, M. H., Gray, H. J., Johnson, J. A. et al. (2015). User guide for luminescence sampling in archaeological and geological contexts. *Adv.Archaeol. Pract.*, 3(2), 166–177.

Nerantzis, N., Kazakis, N. A., Sfampa, I. K. et al. (2017). An integrated approach to the characterization and dating of furnaces in smelting sites in Macedonia, Greece. *JASRep.*, **16**, 65–72. http://dx.doi.org/10.1016/j. jasrep.2017.09.027.

Noll, W., Holm, R. & Born, L. (1975). Painting of ancient ceramics. *Angew. Chem.,Int.Ed.*, **14**(9), 603–613. https://doi.org/10.1002/anie.197506021.

Numrich, M., Schwall, C., Lockhoff, N. et al. (2023). Portable laser ablation sheds light on Early Bronze Age gold treasures in the old world: New insights from Troy, Poliochni, and related finds. *JAS*, **149**, 105694. https://doi.org/ 10.1016/j.jas.2022.105694.

Oniya, E. O., Polymeris, G. S., Tsirliganis, N. C. & Kitis, G. (2012). On the pre-dose sensitization of the various components of the LM-OSL signal of annealed quartz; comparison with the case of 110 °C TL peak. *Radiat. Meas.*, **47**, 864–869. https://doi.org/10.1016/j.radmeas.2012.03.009.

Özkaya, Ö. A. & Böke, H. (2009). Properties of Roman bricks and mortars used in Serapis temple in the city of Pergamon. *Mater.Charact.*, **60**(9), 995–1000. https://doi.org/10.1016/j.matchar.2009.04.003.

Pampuch, R. (2014). *An Introduction to Ceramics*. Cham: Springer.

Papachristodoulou, C., Oikonomou, A., Ioannides, K. & Gravani, K. (2006). A study of ancient pottery by means of X-ray fluorescence spectroscopy, multivariate statistics and mineralogical analysis. *Anal.Chim.Acta*, **573–574**, 347–353. https://doi.org/10.1016/j.aca.2006.02.012.

Papageorgiou, I. (2020). Ceramic investigation: How to perform statistical analyses. *Archaeological and Anthropological Sciences*, **12**, 210. https://doi.org/10.1007/s12520-020-01142-x.

Pappalardo, L. Pappalardo, G., Amorini F. et al. (2008). The complementary use of PIXE-α and XRD non-destructive portable systems for the quantitative analysis of painted surfaces. *X-RaySpectrom.*, **37**(4), 370–375. https://doi.org/10.1002/xrs.1040.

Perlman, I. & Asaro, F. (1969). Pottery analysis by neutron activation. *Archaeometry*, **11**(2), 21–52. https://doi.org/10.1111/j.1475-4754.1969.tb00627.x.

Podoba, R., Stubna, I., Lukovicova, J. & Bacik, P. (2012). The firing temperature of Romanesque Brick from Pác. *J.Civ.Eng.*, **7**, 79–86. https://doi.org/10.2478/v10299-012-0009-y.

Pollard, A. M. & Heron, C. (1996). *Archaeological Chemistry*. Cambridge: Royal Society of Chemistry.

Pollard, A. M., Batt, C. M., Stern, B. & Young, S. M. M. (2007). *Analytical Chemistry in Archaeology*. Cambridge: Cambridge University Press.

Polymeris G. S., Sakalis A., Papadopoulou D. et al. (2007). Firing temperature of pottery using TL and OSL techniques. *NIM-A*, **580**(1), 747–750. https://doi.org/10.1016/j.nima.2007.05.139.

Polymeris, G. S., Kiyak, N. G., Koul, D. K. & Kitis, G. (2014). The firing temperature of pottery from Ancient Mesopotamia, Turkey, using luminescence methods: A case study for different grain-size fractions. *Archaeometry*, **56**(6), 805–817. https://doi.org/10.1111/arcm.12044.

Potter, D. A. (2008). Commercial perspective on the growth and development of the quadrupole ICPMS market. *J.Anal.At.Spectrom.*, **23**, 690–693. https://doi.org/10.1039/B717322A.

Potts, P. (2008). Portable X-ray fluorescence spectrometry: Capabilities for In Situ Analysis. In Potts, P. & West, M., eds., *Portable X-Ray Fluorescence Spectrometry: Capabilities for In Situ Analysis*. Cambridge: RSC, pp. 1–12.

Pradell, T. (2016). Lustre and nanostructures-ancient technologies revisited. In Dillmann, P., Bellot-Gurlet, L. & Nenner I., eds., *Nanoscience and Cultural Heritage*. Dordrecht: Atlantis Press, pp. 3–39. https://doi.org/10.2991/978-94-6239-198-7_1.

Pradell, T. & Molera, J. (2020). Ceramic technology: How to characterize ceramic glazes. *Archaeol.Anthropol.Scis*, **12**, 189. https://doi.org/10.1007/s12520-020-01136-9.

Pradell, T., Molera, J., Roque, J. et al. (2005). Ionic-exchange mechanism in the formation of medieval luster decorations. *JACerS*, **88**, 1281–1289. https://doi.org/10.1111/j.1551-2916.2005.00223.x.

Pradell, T., Molera, J., Smith, A. D., & Tite, M. S. (2008). Early Islamic lustre from Egypt, Syria and Iran (10th to 13th century AD). *J.Archaeol.Sci.* 35(9), 2649–2662. https://doi.org/10.1016/j.jas.2008.05.011

Pradell, T., Molera, J., Salvadó, N. & Labrador, A. (2010). Synchrotron radiation micro-XRD in the study of glaze technology. *Appl.Phys.AMater.Sci. Process.*, **99**, 407–417. https://doi.org/10.1007/s00339-010-5639-7.

Pradell, T., Molina, G., Molera, J., Pla, J. & Labrador, A. (2013). The use of micro-XRD for the study of glaze color decorations. *Appl.Phys.AMater.Sci. Process.*, **111**, 121–127. https://doi.org/10.1007/s00339-012-7445-x.

Pradell, T., Pavlov, R. S., Carolina Gutiérrez, P., Climent-Font, A. & Molera, J. (2012). Composition, nanostructure, and optical properties of silver and silver-copper lusters. *J.Appl.Phys.*, **112**, 054307. https://doi.org/10.1063/1.4749790.

Preusser, F., Chithambo, M., Götte, T. et al. (2010). Quartz as a natural luminescence dosimeter. *EarthSci.Rev.*, **97**, 184–214. https://doi.org/10.1016/j.earscirev.2009.09.006.

Quinn, P. S. (2022). *Thin Section Petrography, Geochemistry and Scanning Electron Microscopy of Archaeological Ceramics*. Oxford: Archaeopress. https://doi.org/10.2307/j.ctv2nwq8x4.

Rambaldi, E., Pabst, W., Gregorová, E., Prete, F. & Bignozzi, M. C. (2017). Elastic properties of porous porcelain stoneware tiles. *Ceram.Int.*, **43**, 6919–6924. https://doi.org/10.1016/j.ceramint.2017.02.114.

Resano, M., Garcia-Riuz, E. & Vanhaecke, F. (2010). Laser ablation – inductively coupled plasma mass spectrometry in archaeometric research. *MassSpectrom.Rev.*, **29**, 55–78. https://doi.org/10.1002/mas.20220.

Rice, P. M. (1987). *Pottery Analysis: A Sourcebook*. Chicago: University of Chicago Press.

Romano, F. P., Pappalardo, L., Masini, N., Pappalardo, G., Rizzo, F. (2011). The compositional and mineralogical analysis of fired pigments in Nasca pottery from Cahuachi (Peru) by the combined use of the portable PIXE-alpha and portable XRD techniques. *Microchem.J.*, **99**(2), 449–453. https://doi.org/10.1016/j.microc.2011.06.020.

Roux, V. (2017). Ceramic manufacture: The chaîne opératoire approach. In Hunt, A., ed., *The Oxford Handbook of Archaeological Ceramic Analysis*. Oxford: Oxford University Press, pp. 101–114.

Roux, V. in collaboration with Courty, M. A. (2019). *Ceramics and Society: A Technological Approach to Archaeological Assemblages*. Cham: Springer Nature. https://doi.org/10.1007/978-3-030-03973-8.

Rueff, B., Debels, P., Vargiolu, R., Zahouani, H. & Procopiou, H. (2021). Reading ceramic surfaces: Characterisation of surface treatments towards functional identification of vases. *JASRep*. **38**, 103021. https://doi.org/10.1016/j.jasrep.2021.103021.

Salinas, E. & Pradell, T. (2020). Madīnat al-Zahrā' or Madīnat Qurtuba? First evidences of the Caliphate tin glaze production of 'verde y manganeso' ware. *Archaeol.Anthropol.Sci.*, **12**, 207. https://doi.org/10.1007/s12520-020-01170-7.

Salinas, E., Pradell, T. & Tite, M. (2019). Tracing the tin-opacified yellow glazed ceramics in the wester Islamic world: The findings at Madīnat al-Zahrā'. *Archaeol.Anthropol.Sci.*, **11**, 777–787. https://doi.org/10.1007/s12520-017-0562-x.

Salinas, E., Reynolds, P. & Pradell, T. (2022). Technological changes in the glazed wares of northern Tunisia in the transition from Fatimid to Zirid rule. *Archaeol.Anthropol.Sci.*, **14**, 224. https://doi.org/10.1007/s12520-022-01690-4.

Sanger, M. C. (2016). Investigating pottery vessel manufacturing techniques using radiographic imaging and computed tomography: Studies from the Late Archaic American Southeast. *JASRep*, **9**, 586–598. https://doi.org/10.1016/j.jasrep.2016.08.005.

Sanjurjo-Sánchez, J., Gómez-Heras, M. & Polymeris, G. S. (2013). Estimating maximum tempe-ratures attained during fires in building stoneworks by thermoluminescence: A case study from Uncastillo, Saragossa (Spain). *MAA*, **13**, 145–153. http://hdl.handle.net/10261/115402.

Sanjurjo-Sanchez, J., Montero Fenollos, J. L. & Polymeris, G. S. (2018). Technological aspects of Mesopotamian Uruk pottery: Estimating firing temperatures using mineralogical methods, thermal analysis and luminescence techniques. *Archaeol.Anthropol.Sci.*, **10**, 849–864. https://doi.org/10.1007/s12520-016-0409-x.

Scarpelli, R., Clark, R. J. H. & De Francesco A. M. (2014). Archaeometric study of black-coated pottery from Pompeii by different analytical techniques. *Spectrochim.ActaPart A*, **120**, 60–66. https://doi.org/10.1016/j.saa.2013.09.139.

Schiffer, M. B. (1990). The influence of surface treatment on heating effectiveness of ceramic vessels. *JAS*, **17**, 373–381. https://doi.org/10.1016/0305-4403(90)90002-M.

Schiffer, M. B., Skibo, J. M., Boelke, T. C., Neupert, M. A. & Aronson, M. (1994). New perspectives on experimental archaeology: Surface treatments and thermal response of the clay cooking pot. *Am. Antiq.*, **59**(2), 197–217. https://doi.org/10.2307/281927.

Schmandt-Besserat, D. (1977). The earliest uses of clay in Syria. *Expedition*, **19**(3), 28–42.

Schramm, R. (2012). *X-Ray Fluorescence Analysis: Practical and Easy*. Bedburg-Hau: Fluxana.

Schwedt, A., Mommsen, H., Zacharias, N. & Buxeda i Garrigós, J. (2006). Analcime crystallization and compositional profile – comparing approaches to detect post-depositional alteration in archaeological pottery. *Archaeometry*, **48**, 237–251. https://doi.org/10.1111/j.1475-4754.2006.00254.x.

Sciau, P., Sanchez, C. & Gliozzo, E. (2020). Ceramic technology: How to characterize terra sigillata ware. *Archaeol.Anthropol.Sci*, **12**, 211. https://doi.org/10.1007/s12520-020-01137-8.

Seman, S., Dussubieux, L., Cloquet, C. & Pryce, T. (2020). Strontium isotope analysis in ancient glass from South Asia using portable laser ablation sampling. *Archaeometry*, **63**(1), 88–104. https://doi.org/10.1111/arcm.12618.

Sharratt, N., Golitko, M. & Williams, P. R. (2015). Pottery production, regional exchange, and state collapse during the Middle Horizon (A.D. 500–1000): LA-ICP-MS analyses of Tiwanaku pottery in the Moquegua Valley, Peru. *J. FieldArchaeol.*, **40**, 397–412. https://doi.org/10.1179/2042458214Y.0000000001.

Shoval, S. (2017). The application of LA-ICP-MS, EPMA and Raman micro-spectroscopy methods in the study of Iron Age Phoenician Bichrome pottery at Tel Dor. *JASRep.*, **21**, 938–951. https://doi.org/10.1016/j.jasrep.2017.03.040.

Shoval, S. & Gilboa, A. (2016). PXRF analysis of pigments in decorations on ceramics in the East Mediterranean: A test-case on Cypro-Geometric and Cypro-Archaic Bichrome ceramics at Tel Dor, Israel. *JASRep.*, **7**, 472–479. https://doi.org/10.1016/j.jasrep.2015.08.011.

Shoval. S., Beck, P., Kirsch, Y. et al. (1991). Rehydroxylation of clay minerals and hydration in ancient pottery from the 'land of Geshur'. *J.Therm.Anal.*, **37**, 1579–1592. https://doi.org/10.1007/BF01913490.

Shugar, A. N. & Mass, J. L. (2014). *Handheld XRF for Art and Archaeology*. Ithaca: Cornell University Press.

Sinopoli, C. M. (1991). *Approaches to Archaeological Ceramics*. New York: Plenum press.

Skibo, J. M., Schiffer, M. B. & Reid, K. C. (1989). Organic-tempered pottery: An experimental study. *Am.Antiq.*, **54**(1), 122–146. https://doi.org/10.2307/281335.

Skibo, J. M., Butts, T. C. & Schiffer, M. B. (1997). Ceramic surface treatment and abrasion resistance: An experimental study. *JAS*, **24**, 311–317. https://doi.org/10.1006/jasc.1996.0115.

Soffer, O., Adovasio, J. M. & Hyland, D. C. (2000). The 'Venus' Figurines. *Curr.Anth.*, **41**(4), 511–537. https://doi.org/10.1086/317381.

Speakman, R. J. & Neff, H. (2002). Evaluation of painted pottery from the Mesa Verde region using laser ablation inductively coupled plasma-mass spectrometry (LA-ICP-MS). *Am.Antiq.*, **67**(1), 137–144. https://doi.org/10.2307/2694882.

Spencer J. Q. G. & Sanderson D. C. W. (2012). Decline in firing technology or poorer fuel resources? High-temperature thermoluminescence (HTTL) archaeothermometry of Neolithic ceramics from Pool, Sanday, Orkney. *JAS*, **39**, 3542–3552. https://doi.org/10.1016/j.jas.2012.05.036.

Sterba, J. H. (2018). A workflow for neutron activation analysis of archaeological ceramics at the Atominstitut in Vienna, Austria. *J.Radioanal.Nucl. Chem.*, **316**, 753–759. https://doi.org/10.1007/s10967-018-5803-7.

Sunta, C. M. & David, M. (1982). Firing temperature of pottery from pre-dose sensitization of TL. *PACT*, **6**, 460–467.

Tema, E., Hatakeyama, T., Ferrara, E. et al. (2024). Insights on the firing temperature of ancient ceramic coffins through a multi-analytical approach: The case of the Sada Nishizuka Kofun, Japan. *J.Cult.Herit.*, **66**, 265–270. https://doi.org/10.1016/j.culher.2023.11.022.

Thér, R. (2016). Identification of pottery forming techniques using quantitative analysis of the orientation of inclusions and voids in thin sections. *Archaeometry*, **58**, 222–238. https://doi.org/10.1111/arcm.12166.

Thér, R. (2020). Ceramic technology: How to reconstruct and describe pottery-forming practices. *Archaeol. Anthropol. Scis*, **12**, 172. https://doi.org/10.1007/s12520-020-01131-0.

Thomas, R. (2013). *Practical Guide to ICP-MS: A Tutorial for Beginners* (3rd Ed.). Roca Raton: CRC Press.

Tite, M. S. (1992). The impact of electron microscopy on ceramic studies. *Proceedings of the British Academy*, **22**, 111–131.

Tite, M. S. (2008). Ceramic production, provenance and use – A review. *Archaeometry*, **50**(2), 216–231. https://doi.org/10.1111/j.1475-4754.2008.00391.x.

Tite, M. S. & Maniatis, Y. (1975). Scanning electron microscopy of fired calcareous clays. *Trans.J.Br.Ceramic.Soc.*, **74**(1), 19–22.

Tite, M. S., Freestone, I., Mason, R. et al. (1998). Lead glazes in antiquity – Methods of production and reasons for use. *Archaeometry*, **40**, 241–260. https://doi.org/10.1111/j.1475-4754.1998.tb00836.x.

Tite, M. S., Kilikoglou, V. & Vekinis, G. (2001). Strength, toughness and thermal shock resistance of ancient ceramics and their influence on technological choices. *Archaeometry*, **43**(2), 301–324. https://doi.org/10.1111/1475-4754.00019.

Tite, M., Shortland, A. & Paynter, S. (2002). The beginnings of vitreous materials in the Near East and Egypt. *Acc.Chem.Res.*, **35**(8), 585–593. https://doi.org/10.1021/ar000204k.

Tite, M., Watson, O., Pradell, T. et al. (2015). Revisiting the beginnings of tin-opacified Islamic glazes. *JAS*, **57**, 80–91. https://doi.org/10.1016/j.jas.2015.02.005.

Trindade, M. J., Dias, M. I., Coroado, J. & Rocha, F. (2009). Mineralogical transformations of calcareous rich clays with firing: A comparative study between calcite and dolomite rich clays from Algarve, Portugal. *Appl. ClaySci.*, **42**, 345–355. https://doi.org/10.1016/j.clay.2008.02.008.

Ul-Hamid, A. (2018). *A Beginners' Guide to Scanning Electron Microscopy.* Cham: Springer Nature. https://doi.org/10.1007/978-3-319-98482-7.

Vandenabeele, P. & Donais, M. K. (2016). Mobile spectroscopic instrumentation in archaeometry research. *Appl.Spectrosc.*, **70**(1), 27–41. https://doi.org/10.1177/0003702815611063.

Vandenabeele, P., Edwards, H. G. & Moens, L. (2007). A decade of Raman spectroscopy in art and archaeology. *Chem. Rev.*, **107**, 675–686. https://doi.org/10.1021/cr068036i.

Vekinis, G. & Kilikoglou, V. (1998). Mechanical performance of quartz-tempered ceramics: Part II, Hertzian strength, wear resistance and applications to ancient ceramics. *Archaeometry*, **40**(2), 281–292. https://doi.org/10.1111/j.1475-4754.1998.tb00838.x.

Velde, B. & Druc, I.C. (1999). *Archaeological Ceramic Materials: Origin and Utilization.* Heidelberg: Springer.

Vieillevigne, E., Guibert, P. & Bechtel, F. (2007). Luminescence chronology of the medieval citadel of Termez, Uzbekistan: TL dating of bricks masonries. *JAS*, **34**, 1402–1416.

Wagner, G. A. (1998). *Age Determination of Young Rocks and Artifacts: Physical and Chemical Clocks in Quaternary Geology and Archaeology.* Berlin-Heidelberg: Springer – Verlag.

Walton, M. S. & Tite, M. S. (2010). Production technology of roman lead-glazed pottery and its continuance into late antiquity. *Archaeometry*, **52**, 733–759. https://doi.org/10.1111/j.1475-4754.2009.00506.x.

Watson, I. A. & Aitken, M. J. (1985). Firing temperature analysis using the 110°C peak of quartz. *Nuclear Tracks*, **10**(4–6), 517–520.

Weigand, P. C., Harbottle, G. & Sayre, E. V. (1977). Turquoise sources and source analysis: Mesoamerica and the southwestern U.S.A. In Earle, T. K. & Ericson, J. E., eds., *Exchange Systems in Prehistory*. New York: Academic, pp. 15–34.

Weyl, W. A. (2016). *Coloured Glasses*. Sheffield: Society of Glass Technology.

Williams, P. R., Sharratt, N., Banikazemi, C. et al. (2023). Ceramic production in the Tiwanaku sphere: LA-ICP-MS in the Moquegua, Titicaca, and Cochabamba regions. *JASRep.*, **50**, 103874. 10.htttps://doi.org/10.1016/j.jasrep.2023.103874.

Wopenka, B., Popelka, R., Pasteris, J. D. & Rotroff S. (2002). Understanding the mineralogical composition of ancient Greek pottery through Raman microprobe spectroscopy. *Appl.Spectrosc.*, **56**, 1320–1328.

Yuan, M., Hou, J., Gorni, G. et al. (2022). Jun ware glaze colours: An X-ray absorption spectroscopy study. *J.Eur.Ceram.Soc.*, **42**(6), 3015–3022. https://doi.org/10.1016/j.jeurceramsoc.2022.02.016.

Ziemann, M. A. & Madariaga, J. M. (2020). Applications of Raman spectroscopy in art and archaeology. *J.RamanSpectrosc.*, **52**, 8–14. https://doi.org/10.1002/jrs.5571.

Zienkiewicz, O. C., Taylor, R. L. & Zhu, J. Z. (2005). *The Finite Element Method: Its Basis and Fundamentals* (6th Ed.). Amsterdam: Elsevier Butterworth-Heinemann. https://doi.org/10.1016/C2009-0-24909-9.

Zimmerman, J. (1971). The radiation induced increase of the 110 °C TL sensitivity of fired quartz. *J.Phys.C:SolidStatePhys.*, **4**(18), 3265–3276. https://doi.org/10.1088/0022-3719/4/18/032.

Cambridge Elements

Current Archaeological Tools and Techniques

Hans Barnard
Cotsen Institute of Archaeology

Hans Barnard was associate adjunct professor in the Department of Near Eastern Languages and Cultures as well as associate researcher at the Cotsen Institute of Archaeology, both at the University of California, Los Angeles. He currently works at the Roman site of Industria in northern Italy and previously participated in archaeological projects in Armenia, Chile, Egypt, Ethiopia, Italy, Iceland, Panama, Peru, Sudan, Syria, Tunisia, and Yemen. This is reflected in the seven books and more than 100 articles and chapters to which he contributed.

Willeke Wendrich
Polytechnic University of Turin

Willeke Wendrich is Professor of Cultural Heritage and Digital Humanities at the Politecnico di Torino (Turin, Italy). Until 2023 she was Professor of Egyptian Archaeology and Digital Humanities at the University of California, Los Angeles, and the first holder of the Joan Silsbee Chair in African Cultural Archaeology. Between 2015 and 2023 she was Director of the Cotsen Institute of Archaeology, with which she remains affiliated. She managed archaeological projects in Egypt, Ethiopia, Italy, and Yemen, and is on the board of the International Association of Egyptologists, Museo Egizio (Turin, Italy), the Institute for Field Research, and the online UCLA Encyclopedia of Egyptology.

About the Series

Cambridge University Press and the Cotsen Institute of Archaeology at UCLA collaborate on this series of Elements, which aims to facilitate deployment of specific techniques by archaeologists in the field and in the laboratory. It provides readers with a basic understanding of selected techniques, followed by clear instructions how to implement them, or how to collect samples to be analyzed by a third party, and how to approach interpretation of the results.

COTSEN INSTITUTE OF
ARCHAEOLOGY AT UCLA

Cambridge Elements

Current Archaeological Tools and Techniques

Elements in the Series

Archaeological Mapping and Planning
Hans Barnard

Mobile Landscapes and Their Enduring Places
Bruno David, Jean-Jacques Delannoy and Jessie Birkett-Rees

Cultural Burning
Bruno David, Michael-Shawn Fletcher, Simon Connor, Virginia Ruth Pullin, Jessie Birkett-Rees, Jean-Jacques Delannoy, Michela Mariani, Anthony Romano and S. Yoshi Maezumi

Knowledge Discovery from Archaeological Materials
Pedro A. López-García, Denisse L. Argote, Manuel A. Torres-García and Michael C. Thrun

Machine Learning for Archaeological Applications in R
Denisse L. Argote, Pedro A. López-García, Manuel A. Torres-García and Michael C. Thrun

Worked Bone, Antler, Ivory, and Keratinous Materials
Adam DiBattista

Infrared Spectroscopy of Archaeological Sediments
Michael B. Toffolo

Retrospective and Prospective for Scientific Provenance Studies in Archaeology
A.M. Pollard

Archaeological Wood and Woodworking
Caroline Arbuckle MacLeod

Bioarchaeology of Infants and Children
L. Creighton Avery

Ceramic Analysis: Laboratory Methods
Irmgard Hein, Mustafa Kibaroğlu, Michaela Schauer, Anno Hein, Georgios S. Polymeris, Judit Molera and Trinitat Pradell

A full series listing is available at: www.cambridge.org/EATT

For EU product safety concerns, contact us at Calle de José Abascal, 56–1°, 28003 Madrid, Spain or eugpsr@cambridge.org.

www.ingramcontent.com/pod-product-compliance
Ingram Content Group UK Ltd.
Pitfield, Milton Keynes, MK11 3LW, UK
UKHW020643041025
463523UK00019B/719